T0165521

ABRAHAM LINCOLN ASCENDENT

ABRAHAM LINCOLN ASCENDENT

The Story of the Election of 1860

Garry Boulard

iUniverse, Inc.
Bloomington

Abraham Lincoln Ascendent
The Story of the Election of 1860

Copyright © 2011 by Garry Boulard

All rights reserved. No part of this book may be used or reproduced by any means, graphic, electronic, or mechanical, including photocopying, recording, taping or by any information storage retrieval system without the written permission of the publisher except in the case of brief quotations embodied in critical articles and reviews.

iUniverse books may be ordered through booksellers or by contacting:

iUniverse
1663 Liberty Drive
Bloomington, IN 47403
www.iuniverse.com
1-800-Authors (1-800-288-4677)

Because of the dynamic nature of the Internet, any web addresses or links contained in this book may have changed since publication and may no longer be valid. The views expressed in this work are solely those of the author and do not necessarily reflect the views of the publisher, and the publisher hereby disclaims any responsibility for them.

Any people depicted in stock imagery provided by Thinkstock are models, and such images are being used for illustrative purposes only.

Certain stock imagery © Thinkstock.

ISBN: 978-1-4620-1540-5 (sc)
ISBN: 978-1-4620-1541-2 (e)

Printed in the United States of America

iUniverse rev. date: 08/19/2011

For Meg and Charlie

ACKNOWLEDGEMENTS

As with my previous books, *Abraham Lincoln Ascendant—The Story of the Election of 1860,* could not have been written without the timely help and assistance of a large number of librarians and archivists, including Andrea Anesi, research assistant, Susquehanna County Historical Society; Christine Beauregard, senior librarian, New York State Library; Kimberly Brownlee, manuscripts librarian, Ward M. Canady Center for Special Collections, University of Toledo; Robert J. Coomer, director, Illinois Historic Preservation Agency; Suzanne Hahn, director, reference services, Indiana Historical Society; Molly Kodner, associate archivist, Missouri Historical Society; Lisa Long, reference archivist, Ohio Historical Society; Curtis Mann, director, Sangamon Valley Collection, Springfield Public Library; Meg McDonald, interlibrary loan specialist, Albuquerque Public Library; Cheryl Schnirring, curator of manuscripts, Abraham Lincoln Presidential Library; Jessica Tyree, research assistant, Southern Historical Collection, University of North Carolina at Chapel Hill; Portia Vescio, public services archivist, University Archives & Historical Collections, Michigan State University; and Jessica Westphal, reference assistant, Special Collections Research Center, the University of Chicago Library.

A special word of thanks to Arsenio Alfredo Baca, Brian Baker, Charles Crago, Sebastian Gomez, Will Griebel, Heyder Magalhmes, Megumi "Meg" Miyajima and Walker Williamson for their friendship and enlightened conversation during the writing of this book; and Peter Arathoon for the cover design.

CHAPTER ONE

———

Between Opposing and Enduring Forces

On December 5, 1859, a bright Monday morning, young John Sherman, tall, thin and slightly whiskered, entered the U.S. Capitol at the head of a revolution.

Elected to Congress at the age of 30 from a wind-swept Ohio district hugging the shores of Lake Erie, Sherman now stood at the age of 35 on the precipice of national power, leading a phalanx of equally young reformers determined to right what they viewed as the dangerously wrong path America was traveling.

"You are mistaken about the Republican party," Sherman had remonstrated with his brother William Tecumseh two years earlier when challenged with the idea that any party based nearly entirely on opposing slavery was doomed to failure. "There are no signs of disunion in its rank," he said of the new organization. "It is now the most compact and by far the strongest political element in our politics."[1]

And this was before the young Republican sweep of the important 1858 mid-term elections, bringing to Congress such firebrands as the rawly athletic 30 year-old Roscoe Conkling of New York, the confrontational 39 year-old Charles Gooch of Massachusetts, and returning for his second term, the amiable 36 year-old Indiana journalist Schuyler Colfax, a close personal friend of Sherman who in the summer of 1859 advised another emerging Republican, Abraham Lincoln: "Nothing is more evident than that there is an ample number of voters in the Northern states opposed to the extension & aggressions of slavery."

But less confident than Sherman that the Republicans would soon take over the country, Colfax also told Lincoln: "It is equally evident, making up this majority, are men of all shades & gradations of opinion."[2]

Those opinions were generously represented by the nearly one hundred new Republican members elected to the House over the span of the previous four years. They came primarily from the small mill towns of western Massachusetts, the rolling countryside of upstate New York, and the flat and mostly unsettled farmland of Ohio, Michigan and Indiana.

And they did indeed represent all shades and gradations of opinion concerning the one issue that dominated all public discourse in the late 1850s: slavery.

Some were for doing away with it immediately; others hoped that pro-slavery militants in the South would eventually succeed in separating the region from the rest of the country, thus finally making America slave-free; while yet a third group believed that simple economics would eventually force

Southerners to reconsider the cost of housing, feeding and clothing 3.2 million slaves, abandoning the system for a less expensive means of crop production that would include free labor.

But what the new Republican members agreed upon completely was prohibiting slavery from expanding into any territories or states in the new West.

"If slavery be a blessing, hug it to your bosoms," one of the new breed, William Kellogg of Illinois, declared on the House floor. "If it burns, scathes, eats out your vitals, it is your own fault and not mine; and you only must work out the remedy for this great evil."

But try and haul slavery into the newest parts of the country, and the young Republicans would "prevent its extension by any and all means."

"We will do it by legislation," warned Kellogg, "We will do it by giving land to the settlers on which to rear the altars and houses of freedom and by cutting off corrupt executive patronage and giving the election of all territorial offices to the people."

His voice rising, Kellogg added: "We will do it by unshackling freedom upon the great Western plains and allowing it to meet there the hideous front of slavery."[3]

It was only natural that men as idealistic as Kellogg, Colfax, Conkling, Gooch and dozens of other young Republicans would turn to John Sherman to carry their banner. It was not because, as Sherman himself would be the first to acknowledge, he displayed any unusual talent for leadership, but primarily because on the issue of preventing slavery's extension he had become such a singular national voice in opposition.

In the spring of 1856, Sherman had cautiously agreed to head up a House committee looking into conditions in Kansas where pro and anti-slavery factions were engaged in an increasingly bloody battle to settle the state with or without slavery.

Sherman and his young wife Margaret Cecilia traveled across Kansas by buggy, exposing themselves, as Sherman later recorded, "to a great deal of fatigue and some danger." But upon the conclusion of his journey, Sherman compiled a report boldly stating that if the administration of President Franklin Pierce would just leave things alone, the Kansas territory would quickly emerge as a "rapid, peaceful and prosperous settlement"--and without slaves.[4]

This conclusion warmed the hearts of anti-slavery advocates across the North who suddenly took note of Sherman. But his next publicity splash, several months later, convinced those same advocates to actively embrace him. Responding to a message from Pierce that made light of troubles in Kansas, Sherman launched an uncharacteristically personal attack against the president who several months before had been denied renomination by his own party, saying that the "Ghost of his defeated hopes haunt him at every step," and that Pierce in his policy towards Kansas had never been anything more than "weak, inefficient, timid and partial."[5]

Sherman later came to regret what he characterized as the "tone and temper" of his anti-Pierce remarks. In fact, Sherman eschewed any exhibit of emotional excess in his public presentations. "In addressing a jury," recalled Sherman, who passed the Ohio bar at the age of 21, "I rarely attempted flights of oratory, and when I did attempt them, I failed. I soon learned that it was better to gain the confidence of a jury by plain talk than by rhetoric."

"Subsequently in public life," Sherman continued. "I pursued a like course."[6]

4

Although well regarded as an abundantly capable legislator, Sherman also doubted his growing reputation as an expert on any number of issues, once telling William Tecumseh of an appearance he made before a group of New York bankers who "waded through a financial speech I made," and strangely "got the idea that I knew ten times more about 'Finance' than I do."[7]

Yet the young Republicans, looking at Sherman's undeniable ability to tackle such complicated issues as taxation, tariffs and governmental expenditures, decided that Sherman had all the makings of a collected and calm leader and should be the next Speaker of the U.S. House.

In a more normal time, the idea of John Sherman as Speaker would have made perfect sense. It wasn't just that he was articulate and interested in policy, he had also made a point of reaching out to all political factions: obviously his fellow young Republicans, but also the cautious Northern Democrats (many of whom were also opposed to slavery but loathe to start a fight with their Southern Democratic counterparts); and to a degree even the slave-holding Southerners.

But these were not normal times. Just four days before the opening of the 1ˢᵗ session of the 39ᵗʰ Congress the nation was riveted by the execution in Charleston, Virginia of the militant abolitionist John Brown, who, with a small band of men, had attacked a federal arsenal in Harper's Ferry, Virginia.

Brown's goal, as he later calmly stated, had been to free all of Virginia's slaves by means of a mass mutiny. If white slave owners died in the process, so be it. Brown, partially financed by Northern money, had long ago come to the conclusion that simply talking about slavery in America was no longer enough. "Moral suasion is hopeless," he declared.

"I don't think the people of the slave states will ever consider the subject of slavery in its true light," Brown continued, "until some other argument is resorted to than moral suasion."[8]

It was inevitable that the Brown incursion, up against a detachment of U.S. Marines, would fail. It was also inevitable that Brown and his men who survived the battle of the arsenal would be quickly sentenced to death.

What surprised many was the response from both those who sympathized with the Southern cause as well as the South itself. Former president Pierce, touted as a possible candidate for the 1860 Democratic nomination because it was thought he could unite the Northern and Southern wings of the party, remarked that it was not what he characterized as the "recent invasion of Virginia," that should cause apprehension, but rather "the teachings, still vehemently persisted in, from which it sprung"--in other words, Republican abolitionism.

The Southern press rallied behind Pierce, with the *New Orleans Daily Delta* calling him "one of those true men who amid all the political aberrations of New England can always be reliably looked to for the maintenance of the constitutional rights of every section of the union."[9]

But this was just about the only good thing that the Southern papers had to say about anyone in the aftermath of John Brown. More typically, Southern columnists exhibited a dangerous anxiety: "It is impossible to conceive an undertaking involving more horrible consequences to society, even if partially successful, than their's," wrote the *Richmond Whig* of Brown and his men. "The gallows never felt the weight of culprits whose lives were more justly forfeit."[10]

As Brown was being led to those gallows, Southerners got even more nervous, worrying that he might be spirited off by a larger and better organized group of militants: "The rumors of intended rescue," reported the *Charleston Daily Courier,* putting up a brave front, are "altogether an egregious hoax." The *New Orleans Bee* cautioned against the "awful pother which has been raised" over the possibility of slaves rising en masse in protest of Brown's execution, hoping that the "supersensitive sons of the Old Dominion will calm their excited nerves."[11]

In fact, Southern slaveholders in general were entirely apoplectic in the days leading up to Brown's hanging. Nervously they wondered: did their own slaves know about Brown's invasion? And if so, were they planning, by cover of night, insurrections of their own? Even the fact that Virginia promised to keep Brown heavily guarded up to the moment of his death was debated, with the *Mobile Daily Register* wondering about Brown's likely martyrdom: "Is this not glory? Is it not enough to start 10,000 weak-minded men into abolition forays on the South?"[12]

In response, also on December 5, Southern House Democrats decided that only a Southern Democrat as Speaker could understand their problems. That afternoon they nominated the moderate Thomas Bocock of Virginia for the job. Because not all of the members had yet to report, 115 votes were needed to win, and on the first ballot Bocock started out strong with 86 votes.

But the important news for the Republicans was the total for Sherman, with 66 votes, and the 43 votes for the 37 year-old Republican Galusha Grow of Pennsylvania. As soon as the balloting concluded, Grow took himself out of the running. Reporters naturally concluded that all of Grow's supporters would swing over to Sherman, leaving him just six votes shy of victory.[13]

It was a prospect that greatly alarmed the South. After the results of the first ballot were in, the *Daily Picayune* of New Orleans spoke for slaveholders across the region when it warned that a Sherman victory would be the "most significant event yet in the progress of the anti-slavery crusade against the South."[14]

But if anyone thought that this meant the Southerners were resigned to defeat, Representative John Bullock Clark of Missouri showed otherwise when he took to the floor of the House the following afternoon to present evidence of what he described as Sherman's "unfitness for the Speakership."

A pro-slavery man, Clark, 59 years old with a youthful face, dark hair and rimless glasses, had been in the House almost as long as Sherman and like his nemesis was a man of detail. It had been his intention to excoriate Sherman immediately after the first ballot, but James Cameron Allen, the Clerk of the House, was not certain that any other business could be entertained until a Speaker was elected and the House officially organized.

This infuriated Clark: "As an individual member of the House, I claim the right to be heard and I deny the power of the House to deprive me of it," he declared as spectators in the gallery both booed and cheered and other members jumped to their feet, demanding recognition.[15]

Thaddeus Stevens, at 67, was hardly a part of Sherman's youthful brigade. He had served in the Pennsylvania legislature when Sherman was just a 10 year-old boy and early on developed what his critics characterized as a dangerous radical agenda that included support for free public education and labor unions. On the issue of slavery, Stevens, who lived with an African-American woman thought to be his mistress, was far ahead of most of his younger Republican counterparts, believing not only that slaves should be freed, but also made full citizens of the country.

Also elected in the Republican wave of 1858, Stevens had served an earlier two terms in the House as a member of the declining Whig party and understood parliamentary procedure better than most of the younger Sherman team.

After Clark made his demand to speak, Stevens, beneath an unconvincing red wig, agreed with Clerk Allen that no other business could be taken up. But already knowing what Clark wanted to talk about, Stevens admonished the younger Republicans who were heading for the doors, noting: "These things must come out and they might just as well come out now."[16]

Even so, it was not until the following afternoon that Clark was able to speak without challenge, and when he did, he galvanized the House as well as the country at large by what he said.

Handing Allen a letter, Clark at first was quiet as the document was read out loud to the House. The letter in question was a circular signed by a large majority of the young Republicans, including most conspicuously Sherman, recommending that a booked entitled *The Impending Crisis of the South* be reprinted and distributed across the North as a Republican party document.

The letter, in turn, had been endorsed by the likes of Horace Greeley, the publisher of the powerful anti-slavery *New York Tribune* and New York Republican party organizer Thurlow Weed, among others. It described non-slave-holding whites in the South as "stupid and sequacious," before inviting them to join with Northern abolitionists in a revolution: "Peacefully, if we can, violently if we must," against slaveholders.[17]

The book itself was a scholarly treatise arguing that slavery held the South down economically as well as socially, and that "Slave holders and slave-breeders are downright enemies of their own section."[18]

Because it was written by a Southerner--Hinton Rowan Helper, who was 28 years old at the time of publication and was born and raised in North Carolina--the book's arguments were regarded by many Southerners as being particularly offensive. There were other apostates in the South, most notably the brooding Senator Andrew Johnson of Tennessee, who would one day astonish Frederick Douglass when he declared that the "colored man and his master" kept the poor white man "in slavery by depriving him of fair participation in the labor and productions of the rich land of the country."[19]

But Helper was substantially more enlightened in his thinking than Johnson. Raised in a family of moderate income— but hardly dirt poor as his detractors asserted—Helper came to the abolitionist cause by a curious route. He had written a book when he was 26 years old called *The Land of Gold*, which took a satirical look at the gold rush in California.

Briefly in that book Helper had attacked Southern slavery, but was forced to excise the critical excerpts when his publisher, a pro-slavery Virginian, objected. Because Helper had already invested $400 of his own money to get the book published, he capitulated, removing all anti-slavery sentiments from the *Land of Gold*. But he greatly resented being censored.

Never particularly worked up about the issue of slavery in the way of a Thaddeus Stevens, Helper quickly came to see the system as corrupt because it also crushed the right of freedom of speech. Southern papers were full of stories of Northern travelers carrying with them anti-slavery literature and being warned to leave at the risk of death. Helper also knew that abolitionist newspapers and books found in the South were regularly destroyed.

Searching for answers, Helper shortly made a bold move by rejecting the Democratic party that ran virtually everything in the South and joining the young Republicans. In 1856 he even campaigned for the dashing 43 year-old Charles Fremont, the Republican nominee for president whose name failed to appear on a single Southern state ballot.

Upon the release of the *Impending Crisis* in 1858, which he dedicated to the "non-slave holding whites of the South," Helper was generally excoriated throughout the South and especially by the Southern members in Congress, who regarded him as a traitor to his own region. And the more they complained, the more books Helper sold and his fame and popularity in the North grew.[20]

That Helper's book should now become a major factor in the election of the next Speaker only hardened attitudes about him in both sections.

As Clark rose to speak, he instantly won the full attention of the House, including transfixed spectators in the gallery who had spent the previous evening wondering what he was going to say.

Now he asked: "Has it come to this?" noting that the North was openly advising non-slave-holding white Southerners to "rise in rebellion," and to do so, "peaceably if they can, forcibly if they must.

Clark started out on solid legal ground, asserting that: "Such advice is treason; such advice is rebellion." In essence, contended the Missouri Representative, the North was waging war on the South.

It must be so, he continued, because this was what Helper's book appeared to suggest and very much what the militant letter signed by Sherman, Greeley and the others was obviously promoting.

Northerners, abolitionists, but particularly the young Republicans, were embracing a deadly philosophy that could ultimately come to no good, thundered Clark: "Wait not to strike the blow, now is the time; now is the day of salvation— strike now. Your arms will be powerless unless you strike the first blow."

"That is the recommendation," continued Clark, "that is the advice. And I say it is advice to revolution. I say it is an incipient movement of treason against a common country."

Although he did not mention Sherman by name, there was no doubt who he was talking about when he added: "What is further asked in that book recommended by these gentlemen? What is asked by the gentleman who is nominated now to preside over this House as Speaker and expects to be elected by the assistance of representatives from slaveholding constituencies?"

It was a good question.

Sherman could not be elected without votes from the South. And now that the facts of his association with Helper's book were in the open, how could any Southerner vote to make Sherman the next Speaker? "Is there one?" Clark asked, somewhat ominously, of any Southern congressman who would now dare to back Sherman. "If there is such a one, I do not envy his situation, nor do I envy the constituency that would sustain him in such a deed."[21]

Clark was followed in an obviously coordinated campaign by Henry Burnett of Virginia who suggested: "Let us enter by a solemn vote our condemnation of the public men of the country who are ready and willing to say that they have endorsed this book," at which point John Gilmer of North Carolina offered a resolution saying that it was the "duty of every good citizen of the Union" to resist any attempt to renew the slavery issue, "under whatever shape and color the attempt be made," and that no one should be elected Speaker "whose political opinions are not known to conform to the foregoing sentiments."[22]

Finally Virginia Representative John Millson, who had served in the House since 1849 and had maintained good relations with Sherman, spoke. Angrily, Millson said that anyone who endorsed Helper's book was not fit to be Speaker. But even more, Millson declared dramatically, "One who consciously, deliberately, and of purpose, lent his name and influence to the propagation of such writings is not only not fit to be Speaker, but is not fit to live."[23]

Millson's explosive remarks prompted an outburst of applause and hissing from the gallery. Stunned, Sherman decided that he had no other choice but to respond.

To a hushed House, Sherman began by saying he did not recall endorsing Helper's book, nor had he read it. He then devoted the rest of his remarks to the attacks against him, missing an opportunity to reassure the handful of wavering Southern members that he in no way subscribed to Helper's message.

"Since I have been a member of this House I have always endeavored to cultivate the courtesies and kind relations that are due from one gentleman to another," said Sherman. "I have never addressed to any member such language as I have heard today. I never desire such language to be addressed to me, if I can avoid it."[24]

Sherman's complaints meant nothing to the Southerners who knew a good issue when they saw it. They continued the assault, with Representative Shelton Leake of Virginia calling Sherman the "abolition candidate for the Speakership of this House," and asking "whether we are to elect a man who, while I am here in the discharge of my duties, is stimulating my negroes at home to apply the torch to my dwelling and the knife to the throats of my wife and helpless children."[25]

Sherman tried to reassure Leake. "I am opposed to any interference whatever by the people of the free states with the relations of master and slave in the slave states," he protested. But the moment was lost and Clerk Allen was suddenly confronting a House out of control as members from both sections cursed and shook their fists at one another.[26]

Martin Crawford of Georgia warned that the people of the South would tolerate no interference from the North: "Do this and my life upon it you will see no cowardly shrinking upon our parts." In response, the always-quick Stevens shot back: "That is right. That is the way they have frightened us before. Now you see exactly what it is and what it has always been."

Stevens' remarks brought a rush of members to the well of the House, several of whom moved towards the aging legislator in a threatening manner but stopped short when they encountered the muscular presence of Roscoe Conkling, who jumped to shield Stevens with the sort of smile that suggested he would enjoy nothing more than flattening a Southerner or two.

After Allen made a plea for order, while also admitting that he had no security force to back him up, Stevens watched the Southerners returned to their seats, before joking to Allen: "This was a mere momentary breeze, sir, nothing else."[27]

Although the young Republicans laughed, they ended December 6 perplexed, recognizing that John Sherman's campaign to become Speaker was in grave jeopardy.

Over the next several days two more ballots would be taken with Sherman picking up votes, but still falling short of a majority. He won the pivotal support of Thurlow Weed, who sent a letter to the *New York Evening Post* predicting that the "struggle will result in the election of Mr. Sherman." But then Weed weakened his prediction by rightly judging that Sherman could only emerge triumphant if the House agreed to a plurality vote.[28]

It was clear that the Southern Democrats had no intention of going that route as they knew it would obviously result in Sherman's election. Instead, with their own members divided between Bocock and Gilmer, they decided to just keep the balloting going with the idea that a tired, frustrated Sherman would eventually throw in the towel. A subsequent movement among the Northern Democrats on behalf of John McClernand of Illinois, who was a strong supporter of his state's Senator Stephen Douglas for the 1860 Democratic presidential nomination, also garnered little enthusiasm with the Southerners who remained content to simply defeat Sherman.

As the snowy, cold days rushed towards Christmas, the Southern strategy seemed to be working. On December 14, Sherman won 108 votes. On the 16th, he rose to 111, a number that stayed the same during two more rounds of balloting the next day. Echoing Weed, the *New York Herald* on December 18 predicted that there could be "no prospect of organization until the plurality rule is adopted."[29]

As the voting and lobbying entered its third full week on December 20, insiders began to worry about the House's functionality: staffers could not be paid until the House was officially organized. The members were also going without money, although Sergeant-at-Arms Adam John Glossbrenner was ladling out small amounts of cash to both Republicans and Democrats and keeping a running total that, according to one report, neared $50,000 by Christmas week. At the same time local mail contractors let it be known that unless Congress organized and passed an appropriation to pay them, their services would cease in just a few more weeks.[30]

The Washington correspondent for the *New York Tribune* maintained that there was a "disposition to elect before Christmas if possible," but voting on December 23—the twentieth ballot—actually saw Sherman's total fall to 103. The next day, Sherman took time out to write to William Tecumseh, who had read press account of the congressman endorsing Helper's book and wondered how his younger brother could have gotten himself into such a fix, advising: "I hope you will conduct yourself manfully."[31]

Exhibiting a knack for strategy that would later characterize his controversial command in the field, William Tecumseh added: "Bear with taunts as far as possible, biding your time to retaliate. An opportunity always occurs."[32]

Now Sherman candidly admitted to William Tecumseh that endorsing Helper's book had been a "thoughtless, foolish and unfortunate act." He said that because one-time Democrat and now Republican insider Francis P. Blair, Sr., who owned slaves, spearheaded the committee promoting the *Crisis of the South,* he was assured that "there should be nothing offensive in it."

Realizing fully that his older brother, who was now stationed in Louisiana, had little use for abolitionists, Sherman added: "Everybody knows that the ultra sentiments in the book are as obnoxious to me as they can be to anyone...whether elected or not, I will at a proper time disclaim all sympathy with agrarianism, insurrection and other abominations in the book."[33]

The House adjourned on Christmas Eve with a last ballot showing Sherman down to 100 votes. Sunday was Christmas, giving the Congressmen one day to be with their families, or in some cases, socialize and drink with friends. By the afternoon of Monday, December 26, some were still drinking. Virginia's William Smith, described by a correspondent for the *New York Times* as a "smallish, thin and nervous little man," held the floor for more than an hour, casually slurping egg nog as he spoke, and offering a detailed defense of slavery.[34]

Finally, Labon Moore of Kentucky, who in vain asked Smith to share his egg nog, wondered not only if Smith's speech would ever end, but if the House would adjourn until after New Year's: "Even the negroes have one week of holiday and recreation at Christmas," Moore said to great laughter.[35]

But the proceedings continued. When President James Buchanan sent his annual message to Congress on December 27 it was tabled in the House until a Speaker could be elected. But because the Senate was organized, Buchanan's words were read in that chamber and reprinted in the national press, adding one more voice to the increasingly angry slavery debate.

Never a fan of the abolitionists and a strong defender of the South's right to have slaves, Buchanan at 68 years of age appeared old and disengaged, although a White House New Year's party several days later would show him in good form, amiably chatting and drinking with visitors. Whatever his current condition, Buchanan felt the need to weigh in on John Brown.[36]

Expressing no sympathy for Brown himself and not even a minimal regard for those who were actually slaves, Buchanan said it was not his intention to "refer in detail to the recent sad and bloody occurrences at Harper's Ferry." But he thought nonetheless that the attack was a symptom of an "incurable disease in the public mind, which may break out in still more dangerous outrages, and terminate, at last, in an open war by the North to abolish slavery in the South."[37]

Although the rest of his message would confine itself to budgetary issues and foreign affairs, Buchanan's Harper's Ferry reference won the most newspaper attention, signaling to Southern Congressional members that the current White House incumbent was very much in their corner and obviously wouldn't vote for Sherman either if he were in their shoes.

On December 30, the day after the 24th ballot showing Sherman at 102 votes, Illinois Senator Lyman Trumbull sent an update to the man he hoped would succeed Buchanan, Abraham Lincoln, who was following the reports of the House election closely. "Our friends," wrote Trumbull, who was also trying to organize Republicans in Washington in favor of Lincoln, "have determined to adhere to Sherman to the end, and I doubt not will eventually elect him."[38]

Lincoln, more politically skilled than was generally known, wisely kept his distance from the Speaker election. It was his rival for the Republican presidential nomination, Senator William Seward of New York, who had become so publicly identified with Sherman, loudly endorsing him for the Speakership and now seeing his influence as a candidate measured by whether Sherman failed or succeeded.

Balloting over the New Year's weekend revealed no changes. On January 4 three inches of snow blanketed the city. Young boys on the street hawked the latest copies of the *Crisis of the South* with cries of "A Helper, sir?" "Do you want a Helper?" That same day Sherman's total declined to 101 votes and then rose again to 104 the following day.[39]

Later on the afternoon of January 5 the Democrats briefly put forward the name of the controversial and hefty Clement Vallandigham of Ohio, who had previously expressed support for the Southern cause. John Potter of Wisconsin generated great laughter when he said "The impression is very strong on my mind that Mr. Vallandigham is somewhat mixed up with the John Brown affair."[40]

Vallandigham, who had no stomach for being a leader, quickly took his name out of contention. As he did so he joked that Potter was a "living contradiction to the dictim of Shakespeare that when the brains were out, the man would die."[41]

Although Republicans laughed, they saw the ongoing balloting as anything but funny. It wasn't just that, like the Democrats, they were living on credit at local boarding houses, hotels and taverns, but that the protracted contest was wearing them down. When, on January 8, a rumor made the rounds that Seward was about to abandon Sherman, panic was felt throughout their ranks, a panic that was only doused when an agent for Seward reconfirmed the New Yorker's support, leaving the young Republicans, thought a *New York Herald* reporter, "firmer, if possible, than ever."[42]

Yet outside Washington, Republican support for Sherman was evaporating. On January 10, *Chicago Tribune* publisher Joseph Medill predicted to Lincoln: "It is doubtful whether our folks succeed in electing Sherman." Medill, also a Lincoln man, added that he thought growing political pressure in the

North to finally resolve the matter would eventually force a small minority of House Republicans to abandon ship and "vote with the Democrats, which will hurt us."[43]

But even if the prospects for the Republicans were crumbling, the Democrats remained on the offensive. That same day, Lucius Gartrell of Georgia rose to explore what he said was a larger question in the ongoing contest. "No one regrets more than I do the existing state of things in this hall," Gartrell began. "And yet I have a thorough confidence that the blame of our non-organization can in no way attach to me or to the party with which I am acting."[44]

Other observers of the long process worried that it was making Washington look bad across the country. Andrew Johnson, sometimes slow, hoped there would be a "change for the better before long or it will look like there is a deadlock in the government." But Gartrell said he was more concerned that the continued Republican support for Sherman was in reality part of a larger plot by the young Republicans to tear the nation in two.[45]

"The scenes being enacted here are but the beginning, in a legislative sense, of that accursed 'irrepressible conflict' doctrine of which we of late have heard so much," said Gartrell, a conflict "between opposing and enduring forces, a conflict by the North upon the South."

Saying that it was his desire to speak "candidly, plainly, dispassionately and respectfully," Gartrell added that if war was to come and the "principles of the Republican party are still to be maintained and their purposes accomplished," perhaps it would be better all around "if this House should never be organized."

Gartrell's thesis was simple. By seeking liberty through the destruction of slavery, the young Republicans were hypocrites because in so doing they were also destroying a singular constitutional right of their fellow Americans in the South—and that was the right to own a slave. "The blood of Southern men shed at Harper's Ferry cries to us from the ground and brands you with the acts of the poor, miserable, deluded followers of your misplaced philanthropy. The ghosts of the dead will haunt you and the anathema of the living will follow you forever," he charged.

Gartrell added that it was only ten days into 1860 and already the young Republicans had precipitated "the great issue as to whether the government shall be longer continued."[46]

Gartrell's remarks revealed the suspicion, as maintained by the *Charleston Mercury* on January 11, that the "great majority of Northern states insist on electing to this office of dignity and influence a man who is nothing less than an abolition incendiary."[47]

With nerves increasingly on edge, the atmosphere in the House became electric. Friendships frayed under the pressure, making it almost impossible for casual relationships to endure. Older Southern Democrats daily gathered around a large wooden table on their side of the aisle and regarded with suspicion the Northern Republicans, who responded in kind as they congregated around a table of their own.

On January 12, John Haskin of New York, a one-time Democrat who saw which way the political winds were blowing in 1858 and joined the Republican party, was about to speak when a pistol fell from his breast pocket. It was well known that members of the House often brought weapons with them to the floor and Haskin said he only did so because he had been out late the night before and lived in what he described as a "neighborhood where outrages have been committed."[48]

But his explanation came only after other members, thinking Haskin was about to shoot them, drew their own revolvers. Only after Clerk Allen was once again prevailed upon to beg for order, did things quiet down, at which point Thomas Davidson of Louisiana joked that "if these things are to continue in the future, I must bring a double-barrel shotgun into the House with me."[49]

The appearance of Haskin's gun was regarded by some as a metaphor for the general sense of anarchy that had overtaken the House. The *New York Herald* on January 14 forecast a coming "reign of terror" as the only result of Sherman's election. "The agitation in the South will have more food," the paper predicted," while the reactionary sentiment at the North will increase in speed and intensify." The *Daily Picayune* was equally glum: "The ship of State is in the rapids hurrying to the precipice of disunion, and there is nothing left but to abandon it for the nearest chance of safety."[50]

The *Daily Picayune* obviously spoke for slaveholders in Louisiana and several other Deep South states who subscribed to the famous paper. William Tecumseh Sherman talked with many of those same people. On January 16 he confided to his brother that while he hoped Congress would soon organize, he still worried that a Northern, and hence young Republican domination of the House would usher in a non-stop anti-Southern assault.

"It would be the height of folly to drive the South to desperation," wrote William Tecumseh, "and I hope after the fact is admitted that the North has the majority and right to control national matters and interests, that they will so use their power as to reassure the South that there is no intention to disturb the actual existence of slavery."[51]

At last on January 20 came the conversation that so many members of the House had been waiting to hear. John Bullock Clark stood to explain that when he introduced his resolution on December 6 condemning Sherman he had done so with "no personal ill feeling towards Mr. Sherman, the Republican candidate for Speaker, apart from what I considered to be an improper act of his—namely, the recommendation of that book."

"So far as that affects his political or social character," added Clark, "he must of course bear it."[52]

Seizing the opportunity, Sherman rose to finally deliver a lengthy explanation and defense of himself, criticizing Clark and the Southern Democrats for trying to stir up the slavery issue only for political gain, and once again declaring that he had never taken a public stand on slavery as it currently existed, only as it was proposed to be extended into the new territories.

"I never made but one speech on the subject of slavery," continued Sherman, "and that was in reference to what I regarded as an improper remark made by President Pierce in 1856. I then spread upon the record my opinions on the subject—and I have found no man to call them into question. They are the opinions which I now entertain."[53]

Then, in an announcement which caught everyone by surprise, Sherman said he would withdraw as a candidate, but only when his fellow Republicans found a suitable replacement.

Some Southerners were also beginning to think about forwarding a candidate who, if moderate enough, might be able to get enough Northern votes to win. But within the ranks of the Southern Democratic caucus was a chasm. Some

Southerners wanted to elect one of their own and see the House organized. Others contemplated the idea of closing the whole process down.

"No one can see now how the controversy is to be terminated and the Southern members are fast becoming reconciled to their present unorganized condition," said Mississippi Senator Jefferson Davis in a letter from Washington to his friend, U.S. consul general to Egypt, Edwin De Leon on January 21.

Davis, the acknowledged leader of the slaveholders in the Senate and also a possible candidate for the 1860 Democratic presidential nomination, although he said he favored Franklin Pierce, added: "As we little to hope and much to deprecate from the action of the present congress, no legislation may be our best estate."[54]

Although some Republicans, such as Stevens, who said his support would endure "until the crack of doom," vowed to continue backing Sherman, others began to fish around for a new contender. The *New York Tribune*, whose influence among the young Republicans was unmatched, thought the whole thing a tragedy: "Great injustice has been done to Mr. Sherman and the body of men who have sustained him so gallantly."[55]

Even so, a new candidate had to be found, and the Republicans suddenly appreciated that it could not be a man like Sherman—young, forceful, associated with the national Republican cause and, of course, an endorser of Helper's book. In a party caucus on January 28 they knocked around the idea of William Pennington, a 63-year old Republican from an industrial northern district in New Jersey whose previous political experience was confined to state office and had only entered Congress in 1858 as part of the Republican landslide.

Quickly, as reported by the *Springfield Daily Republican,* a clear majority of the Republicans had "expressed their intention of supporting Mr. Pennington."[56]

But Southerners had reason for hope too, putting forward the name of William N. H. Smith of North Carolina as a moderate who might win Northern votes. From the Senate chamber, Jefferson Davis wrote to Pierce, noting that the Southern Democrats were optimistic, but adding: "So many chickens have been counted from eggs that proved addled that I have no confidence in the prophecies of the House."[57]

That afternoon, Sherman, nearly drowned out by the cries of his fellow Republicans who, at least, decided to make a great, final show of things, announced he was bowing out. But in a last shot at the Southern Democrats he warned the members not to support for Speaker any of the Southerners who "have proclaimed that under any circumstances, or in any event, they would dissolve the union of these states."[58]

Sherman's official exit precipitated a mass Republican swing over to the surprised Pennington. Because now the full House was voting, 117 votes were required to elect a Speaker. On the 40th ballot taken immediately after Sherman's speech, Pennington had 115.

Two more ballots changed nothing, with North Carolina's Smith uniting the Southern Democrats but never overtaking Pennington and making some observers wonder if even without the controversial Sherman in the running the House was doomed to remained unorganized.

As the members readied for an immediate 43rd ballot, Missouri's Clark rose to suggest that the election of Pennington was probably inevitable but was also of no real importance. What really mattered was that Sherman had been rightly flattened:

"That resolution of mine has worked its effect," Clark crowed. "It has smoked out before the American people the fact that an endorser of the Helper book cannot be Speaker of the House."[59]

It would take two more ballots until the forces behind Pennington were able to put him over. When they did, by only one vote, the galleries erupted in applause. Clerk Allen gaveled for order with roughly the same success he had shown in controlling the House before. In a show of unity, Sherman and Bocock escorted Pennington to the Speaker's chair.

Pennington made a nice first impression, remarking: "After witnessing the almost insurmountable obstacles in the way of an organization of this House, I came to the conclusion that any gentleman of any party who could command a majority of votes for Speaker was bound in deference to the public exigencies to accept the responsibility as an act of patriotic duty, whether it was agreeable to his personal feelings or not."[60]

The immediate effect of the Pennington vote meant that the House was finally organized, members and staff were paid and the mail—through a new congressional appropriation—delivered.

But political analysts saw in Pennington's improbable ascension a solid victory for the Southerners and an embarrassing defeat for two presidential front-runners: Republican Seward, who had made so much of his support for Sherman, and Democrat Stephen Douglas, who had loyally boasted John McClernand.

It was also noted that Abraham Lincoln, by wisely staying out of the battle, had at the very least done no harm to his own quiet campaign.

In fact, the Southerners, by simultaneously thwarting the will of both Seward and Douglas, scored a twin victory, regarding as they did the two hated presidential hopefuls as either openly hostile to slavery (Seward) or opposed to its expansion (Douglas).

Pennington's sudden rise changed nothing within the Republican caucus—although, absurdly, reporters now mentioned him, along with Seward and Lincoln, as a possible Republican presidential nominee. Sherman, with a knack for organization, was still regarded as the leader of the House Republicans and calmly put in Pennington's hands a list of men that the new Speaker compliantly appointed to any number of committees.[61]

What was changed was a new hardness of feeling that had been on blazing display between the sections during the Speakership battle. Caleb Cushing, a former attorney general during the Pierce administration and stern critic of the abolitionist movement, warned of a storm that was rapidly approaching. It was a sentiment that Davis thought accurately reflected a darkening national mood.

"I will stand by the flag and uphold the Constitution whilst there is possibility of effecting anything to preserve and perpetuate the govt. we inherited," Davis frankly told Pierce. "Beyond that my duty and my faith binds me to Mississippi and her fortunes as she may shape them."[62]

[23]Ibid, 21.

[24]Ibid.

[25]Ibid.

[26]Ibid.

[27]Ibid. "From Washington," *New York Tribune*, 8 December 1859, p. 6; Ralph Korngold, *Thaddeus Stevens—A Being Darkly Wise and Rudely Great* (New York: Harcourt, Brace and Company, 1955), 102-03; "From Washington," *New York Tribune*, 10 December 1859, p. 5; "Interesting from Washington," *New York Herald*, 10 December 1859, p. 1; "Washington Letter from Thurlow Weed," *New York Herald*, 9 December 1859, p. 2; "Affairs in Washington," *New York Herald*, 14 December 1859, p. 1.

[28]"Affairs in Washington," *New York Herald*, 18 December 1859, p. 1.

[29]"Interesting from Washington," *New York Herald,* 19 December 1859, p. 4; "Washington Letter," *Daily Picayune,* 22 December 1859, p. 2.

[30]"From Washington," *New York Tribune*, 22 December 1860, p. 5; Thorndike, *The Sherman Letters*, 77-78.

[31]*The Sherman Letters,* 77-78.

[32]Ibid., 78-79.

[33]"Egg Nog in Congress," *Baltimore American*, 3 January 1860, p. 2

[34]"Affairs at Washington," *New York Times*, 26 December 1859, p. 1.

[35]*Congressional Globe,* 254.

[36]"The President's New Year Levee," *Baltimore American*, 3 January 1860, p. 1.

[37]"News of the Day," *New York Times*, 28 December 1859, p. 1; John Bassett Moore, *The Works of James Buchanan, Volume X, 1856-1860* (New York: Antiquarian Press, 1960), 339.

[38]Lyman Trumbull to Abraham Lincoln, 30 December 1859, Abraham Lincoln Papers, Reel 5.

[39]"Letter from Washington," *Daily Picayune*, 15 January 1860, p. 3.

[40]*Congressional Globe*, 348.

[41]Ibid.

[42]"Interesting from Washington," *New York Herald*, 9 January 1860, p.1.

[43]Joseph Medill to Abraham Lincoln, 10 January 1860, Abraham Lincoln Papers, Reel 5.

[44]*Congressional Globe*, 388.

[45]Like many across the country, Johnson's son Robert was fascinated by the Speakership battle and asked his father on January 10 to send him copies of the *Congressional Globe* "from the *beginning* of this session, as I want to be fully posted on the election of Speaker & c. [Congress]." Leroy P. Graf, *The Papers of Andrew Johnson, Volume 3, 1858-1860* (Knoxville: University of Tennessee Press, 1972), 379-82; Robert Johnson to Andrew Johnson, 10 January 1860, Andrew Johnson Papers, Series 2, Reel 39.

[46]*Congressional Globe*, 386-93.

[47]"The South in Congress," *Charleston Mercury*, 11 January 1860, p. 1.

[48]*Congressional Globe*, 432-35.

[49]Ibid.

[50]"The Reign of Terror Approaching in the United States," *New York Herald*, 14 January 1860, p. 6; "The Speakership," *Daily Picayune*, 15 January 1860, p. 3.

[51]Thorndike, *The Sherman Letters,* 79.

[52]*Congressional Globe*, 547.

[53]Ibid, 548.

[54]Lynda Lasswell Crist, *The Papers of Jefferson Davis, Volume 6, 1856-1860* (Baton Rouge: Louisiana State University, 1989), Jefferson Davis to Edwin De Leon, 21 January 1860, 270-72.

[55]"From Washington," *New York Tribune*, 25 January 1860, p. 5.

[56]Although Pennington had not endorsed the Helper book, he was strongly opposed to the pro-slavery Lecompton Constitution in Kansas, angrily characterizing it as a "Wholesale violation of the right of suffrage," and asking "Can any man justify such a measure?" "The Ratification Meeting," *Newark Daily Advertiser,* 28 September 1858, p. 2; "From Washington," *Springfield Daily Republican,* 30 January 1860, p. 4.

[57]Jefferson Davis to Franklin Pierce, 30 January 1860, Franklin Pierce Papers, Series 3, Reel 6.

[58]*Congressional Globe,* 634; "Important from Washington," *New York Herald,* 31 January 1860, p. 1. 59. *Congressional Globe,* 641.

[60]*Congressional Globe,* 655; "The Election of Speaker," *Springfield Daily Republican*, 3 February 1860, p. 2.

[61]Sherman, *John Sherman's Recollections*, 179-80.

[62]Jefferson Davis to Franklin Pierce, 30 January 1860, Franklin Pierce Papers, Series 3, Reel 6.

CHAPTER TWO

The Little Giant in a Fix

Three days after his dark letter to Franklin Pierce, Jefferson Davis rose in the Senate to introduce a series of wordy resolutions defining what he thought should be the proper relationship between the states and the federal government.

Slender, intense, quick to anger, yet also surprisingly laconic, Davis was universally regarded as the leader of the Southern die-hards, a "courteous, cultivated man whose wit is a rapier, drawing blood wherever it touches," remarked the *New York Tribune*. He was determined that the South should make clear its expectations and demands in the 1860 election.[1]

In presenting his resolutions, Davis bluntly admitted that he did not want to spark a conversation, something that was almost impossible to avoid in the Senate. Rather, he hoped to obtain a vote on the six resolutions as an "expression of the deliberate opinion of the Senate."

The resolutions failed to break any new philosophical ground, asserting that the states were essentially "free and independent sovereignties," that slavery in the South was protected by the Constitution, and that Congress did not possess the power to deny anyone from taking a slave into a new territory. But in a slap to the young Republicans, Davis also added that it should be left to the people of any new territory or state to "decide for themselves whether slavery as a domestic institution shall be maintained or prohibited within their jurisdiction."[2]

Journalists interpreted the Davis resolutions as a first foray in a possible candidacy for the presidency. But Davis, in that peculiar time-honored American tradition, denied that he was interested in the job. On February 10 he told a correspondent that "I have given less consideration than you suppose to the selection of our candidate for the ensuing Presidential campaign," adding that he was also not "one of those who insist upon a Southern man for the first office."[3]

This was all true to a point. Davis actually was most concerned with making sure that the South took a strong stand within the Democratic party in 1860. In that effort, his resolutions, winning the swift and almost knee-jerk backing of his fellow Southern Democratic senators, were designed to convince the national Democratic party that it must stand up for the South or go down to defeat.

But Davis had indeed been thinking about the Democratic presidential nomination and knew one thing for certain: it should not be awarded to the always-available Stephen Douglas of Illinois, a man who had, thought Davis, waffled so much on the issue of slavery as to be no better than the likes of William Seward or Abraham Lincoln. This was a view widely shared throughout the South, particularly among the governing class, with the *Charleston Mercury* on January 16 describing Douglas as a "Demagogue whose whole aim is to entangle the South in his anti-slavery meshes while gratifying his inordinate personal aspirations."[4]

Yet, despite the open opposition of Davis and other Southern leaders, Douglas during the early months of 1860 was rounding up delegates. He won the support of his native Illinois in January, followed by caucus wins in Ohio, Indiana, Michigan and Minnesota just weeks later. By late March Douglas supporters added Maine, New Hampshire, Vermont and Rhode Island to their totals, although the large New York and Pennsylvania delegations remained uncommitted.[5]

Even so, Douglas' desire to quickly wrap up the Democratic nomination and unite the party behind him was constantly being challenged by events beyond his control. And not just the debate over whether or not slavery should be extended into the new territories, but also, beginning in early March, the disclosures of rampant corruption within the Buchanan administration which had the altogether predictable effect of depressing the enthusiasm of party captains in general.

On the slavery issue, Douglas moved quickly, telling the Senate on January 23—with the galleries once again packed with spectators—that the John Brown invasion was the "natural, logical, inevitable result of the doctrines and teachings of the Republican party," and that slavery would ultimately be protected or prohibited only by a local considerations: "If I were a citizen of Louisiana, I would vote for retaining and maintaining slavery because I believe the good of that people would require it," Douglas declared. "As a citizen of Illinois, I am utterly opposed to it, because our interests would not be promoted by it."[6]

Douglas' remarks brought him immediate criticism from Davis. His stand was the direct product of the "Freeport Doctrine" he revealed while debating Abraham Lincoln in 1858, leaving it up to territory citizens to decide the slavery question for themselves. But Davis, also angry that Douglas opposed the controversial Lecompton Constitution, which would have brought Kansas into the union as a slave state, wanted territory citizens to be allowed to vote on the slavery issue as a precondition to statehood and was naturally for slavery's expansion.

Repeatedly Davis challenged Douglas on the Senate floor in a series of entrapping rejoinders, eventually reducing him to such nuanced minimalism that Davis could humorously if inaccurately observe: "I think between two such patriots there cannot be any difference at all."[7]

A man given to drinking, depression and moments of frightening euphoria, Douglas was 5'4" tall. He was called the "Little Giant" because he seemed larger than he really was. He also seemed older than his 46 years, having been a dominant national political force for most of the last decade. Elected to the U.S. Senate from Illinois in 1847, Douglas—along with James Buchanan—was regarded as a major contender for the Democratic presidential nomination in 1852, but lost out in protracted balloting that saw Franklin Pierce emerge as the surprise winner.

Less than two years later, Douglas ushered through Congress the legislation that probably did more to destroy the young Pierce presidency than anything else: the Kansas-

Nebraska Act, allowing people of the two territories to decide for themselves the slavery issue and by so doing reigniting the explosive slavery debate throughout the country.

When, in the summer of 1856, Pierce was regarded by nervous Democrats as a political liability, Douglas once again tried for the presidential nomination, but lost out to Buchanan, who having served as Pierce's Minister to Great Britain had not been involved in the messy Kansas-Nebraska debate.

Twin defeats on the national stage should have been enough to end for good any hope that Douglas may have still nourished for the White House, but he broke with Buchanan in late 1857 after the new president allied himself with pro-slavery forces in Kansas, and dramatically declared "By God, sir, I made James Buchanan, and by God, I will unmake him." It was a smart move because it made Douglas independent of the White House, establishing him as a power center to whom all other Democrats disgruntled with the Buchanan presidency could rally.[8]

The following year Douglas additionally became a part of national lore when, running for re-election to the Senate, he engaged in a series of intelligent, witty and contentious debates with Lincoln in Illinois that captivated the country. The Lincoln-Douglas debates were picked up by the wire services and reported at length in dozens of newspapers from the East coast to the West, giving Lincoln the exact kind of publicity he would need if he ever hoped to best Seward for the 1860 Republican nomination. But the debates also established Douglas as both the odds-on favorite for the Democratic presidential nomination as well as the prohibitive favorite for the general election in November, if the warring Democrats could remain united for that long.

Because Douglas had become such an unruly force within the party by 1860, the fortunes of other potential candidates depended entirely on whether he could amass enough of a lead by the time of the Democratic convention as to seem unbeatable. James Guthrie of Kentucky, the former treasury secretary under Pierce, and Senator Robert M. T. Hunter of Virginia both emerged as Southern moderates with potential Northern support who might pick up the pieces if Douglas failed. Pierce himself left with his wife on an extended vacation in Nassau, writing to New Hampshire supporter John George on February 17 that he was certain that friends who knew his true feelings would not try to draft him for the presidency: "The last thing they would do would be to consent to the use of my name before the convention."[9]

Running an amateur effort that relied heavily on the advice of a few Tennessee cronies, Andrew Johnson, who disliked Douglas as he did nearly everyone, thought he could be stopped. Johnson also could not shake the feeling that the president, whom he also disliked, secretly wanted to try for another term. But everywhere that Johnson' s men looked it was the pudgy Douglas that they saw on the horizon. In mid-February Henry Wax, a Tennessee supporter, wrote Johnson to report that Douglas "is sending documents to every man in this country, & he is gaining ground every day."[10]

Noting the growing delegate support and organization for Douglas in the Midwest, Detroit lawyer Anthony Ten Eyck wrote Johnson on February 20 and bluntly concluded that the "sentiment is almost universally & determinately in favor of Douglas."[11]

The challenge for Douglas at this point, however, was not simply winning the Democratic nomination, but trying to also bolster the flagging spirits of a party that had won 6 of the last 8 presidential elections. Democrats, Douglas knew, were both tired and inevitably tainted, a fact that John Covode decided to use to his advantage when he rose to speak in the House on March 5.

Covode, who had remained steadfast to John Sherman throughout the protracted balloting for the Speakership, had come to the stunning conclusion that the patronage-ridden, party machine-run Buchanan administration might actually have corruption problems. He proposed that a committee made up of five House members be drawn up to investigate "whether the President of the United States, or any other officer of the government, has by money, patronage or other improper means," tried to influence Congress or use bribes to influence elections, particularly in Buchanan's home state of Pennsylvania.[12]

It was a wide-ranging, amorphous resolution that met with immediate success when Speaker William Pennington, with Sherman's enthusiastic support, appointed what would come to be known as the Covode Committee for the purpose of pinpointing and ferreting out all corruption in the Buchanan administration.

Buchanan wisely sized up the Covode committee as nothing but trouble, but initially proclaimed indifference. He had hosted a lavish White House party at the end of February attended by more than two thousand people and a more intimate dinner during the first week of April, where a correspondent lauded the aging president as "one of the most delightful diners in the world. He has a fund of small talk for the ladies, a variety of old-fashioned anecdotes, and as he is by no means sparing of the juice of the grape, he grows more easy and more affable and more agreeable as the repast goes on."[13]

In between these two happy, liquid events, Buchanan sent in his official and petulant response to the Covode Committee.

Always a stickler for details, Buchanan began by protesting against the very existence of the committee: "The Constitution has invested the House of Representatives with no power, no jurisdiction, no supremacy whatever over the Presidency," Buchanan asserted, although he acknowledged that the House did have the power to impeach.

He then cast doubt on Covode himself: instead of any charges of administration corruption being weighed by the House Committee on the Judiciary, noted the president, the House had "made my accuser one of my judges."

"To make the accuser the judge," Buchanan added, "is a violation of the principles of universal justice and is condemned by the practice of all civilized nations."[14]

Buchanan's protest fell on the deaf ears of his opponents, who had long tired of him, with the *New York Times* characterizing his arguments as a "deplorable exhibition of feminine indignation."[15]

This was hardly the first time that Buchanan, popularly known as "Old Buck," had been likened to a woman. A lifelong bachelor who had shared quarters for more than a decade with the handsome and single William R. King, Senator of Alabama, Buchanan was often criticized for simply being unmarried. Andrew Johnson publicly doubted the judgment of a man "whose bosom has never swelled with emotions for wife or children."[16]

But others found feminine, or at the least, unmanly traits in his oftentimes prissy, exacting personality. In a letter to former president Martin Van Buren on February 13, one-time Washington newspaper editor Frank Blair said that "The country has been cursed with what [Thomas Hart] Benton called Hermaphrodites, and of all, Old Buck has proved the worst."[17]

Buchanan's peculiar flirtations, combined with a parlor love of gossip, was on particular display in a letter he wrote to Robert Tyler on February 21, just as Covode was getting ready to make his sensational charges against the administration.

Tyler, the son of former president John Tyler, was 44 years old. Buchanan, fifteen years older, had long enjoyed a friendship with the younger man, strangely telling Tyler to "talk to me like a father & give some useful instruction to your dutiful son, if you don't intend coming here soon where we could converse with less trouble."

Buchanan then reported recent rumors he had picked up suggesting that a group of well-heeled New Yorkers may have won Pennsylvania for him during the 1856 election. It may have seemed incredible that he knew nothing about this, but Buchanan claimed it was all news to him: "Did New York money & influence turn things so decidedly in 1856 as they represent it?" he asked Tyler, who had served as a party leader in Pennsylvania. "Is it true that any influences that were brought to bear in Penn. then made any material change in what the result would have been?"

Buchanan then oddly instructed the younger man: "I want you to post me up in these things, & I want you to do it at your leisure & not give yourself any trouble, but you know it will never do for you to leave me, your favorite child, in ignorance."[18]

Speculation about Buchanan's private life never hurt him politically. Nor did the charges that his administration was basically lacking in direction and purpose. But the Covode Committee, listening to dozens of witnesses throughout the spring, was substantially more dangerous because it threatened to unveil the unsavory machine politics component to Buchanan's presidency in a way that could conceivably even lead to charges of impeachment.

Rejecting Buchanan's arguments, Sherman ordered the Covode Committee to continue in its work, telling the president, "This House, sir, has the right to examine into anything which may affect the conduct of any public officer under this government."[19]

As the Democrats throughout the spring read of new disclosures that never entirely sunk Buchanan but certainly damaged his already flaccid reputation, their spirits flagged. It was no wonder that they approached their coming nominating convention with loathing.

And the fact that the delegates were set to meet in Charleston, South Carolina, only made things worse.

A city of just over 40,000, Charleston had been selected during the last Democratic convention as the location for the 1860 meet in an attempt to assuage Southerners who had complained that the Democrats always convened in a Northern locale.

But as the date of the convention neared, both delegates and reporters began to openly express doubts that the quaint city was up to handling the demands of hosting a major party meeting. "There will be at least 20,000 strangers present, and the number may possibly be extended to 50,000," warned a reporter for the *New York Herald* in early March. And even if only that 20,000 showed up, the city would be overtaxed: "The hotels and boarding houses of Charleston will hardly accommodate more than 5,000 men."[20]

Delegates also complained that Charleston hoteliers, determined to make a quick buck, were charging more than twice their usual rates, although the *Charleston Courier* defended such increases, arguing that they would prevent overcrowding: "Let the hotel keepers turn an 'honest penny' and serve their country at the same time," said the paper. "Honest members of the convention will not begrudge the contribution levied if it relieves them of lobby loafers."[21]

A meeting of the party's executive committee, also in Charleston, charged with overseeing arrangements for the convention, quickly weighed in, listening to the complaints of Clement Vallandigham, always ready to jump into any controversy, that there was a growing opposition to meeting in the South Carolina city. Vallandigham strongly urged a rescheduling of the convention in a more appropriate locale. That prompted Representative William Barksdale of Mississippi, a friend of Jefferson Davis, to assert that it would be "inexpedient, under existing circumstances, to change the place of holding the next National Democratic Convention from Charleston to any other city."[22]

With the ameliorating support of Douglas man Thomas Dyer of Illinois, who reflected his candidate's desire to keep the South happy at all costs, the committee quickly voted, with little sense of the impending doom, to keep the convention in Charleston.

As the Democratic delegates from around the country learned of the executive committee's decision, the nation's newspapers were devoting increasing space not only to the probable divisions within the Democratic party, but also the country itself. Certainly since the Speaker of the House battle more and more politicians were openly talking about the possibility of the South going its own way. But now with the talk of separation also came talk of a civil war—although no one was sure if things would really come to that. On the night of April 15, a figure from the past re-emerged to warn both his fellow Democrats and Americans in general that such talk was getting out of hand.

John Tyler at 70 was well regarded both in the North and South as a gentleman farmer and a romantically vigorous man who had married when he was 54 years old for the second time, after his first wife died. His new 24 year-old wife would eventually give him seven children in addition to the seven he already had with his first wife.

Leaving the presidency in 1845 after the Democrats nominated James Knox Polk, Tyler retired to his 1,200-acre Virginia plantation, which he called Sherwood Forest, and remained on good terms with all of his successors.

Adroitly, he avoided becoming actively involved in politics in his post-presidential years, but speaking at a dinner at the Exchange Hotel in Richmond upon the unveiling of a statue of Henry Clay, Tyler bluntly stated that it was his desire to "of necessity, speak of Union," a remark that won him a round of applause from the dining Southerners.

Tyler then smoothly transitioned from reminiscing about Clay, whom he said averted the possibility of an earlier civil war when he helped to broker the Compromise of 1850, to the dangers of a similar war in 1860.

"What badge of distinction is proud enough for him who saves his country from civil war?" challenged Tyler. Eloquently he suggested that the answer could be found in the wife of a dead soldier "as she flies to the rock and desert with her infant son strained to her breast and concealed from view by the tresses of her streaming hair."

"Ask brave and stalworth men as they take their position in opposing ranks to shed each other's blood," Tyler continued. "Ask one, ask all, what monument he deserves who drives away this horrible specter of civil war and restores his country to peace and confidence."

Clearly, Tyler did not think that secession and war was anything to joke about, but in case anyone wondered where he stood in the coming election, he added: "I have but little to do with the politics of the present day. Little to do with them, except to wish them safely ended. I have fears, I have doubts, I have settled opinions. But they are my own in the privacy of my retirement."[23]

Less than one week after Tyler's speech, delegates began to arrive in Charleston, many coming by way of steamboat from Boston and Philadelphia. They were hardly unimpressed with their first views of the historic city. The weather was hot with a bright sun beating down on flowers that had been planted in public squares throughout the city. "There are whole streets that look as if they had not been disturbed since the Redcoats paraded along them," noted a *Cincinnati Commercial* reporter who came by rail. "But there are other streets, however, that look decidedly business-like."[24]

Northerners took some time getting used to the large numbers of black people everywhere, making up fully half of Charleston's population. Visiting an open marketplace in downtown Charleston, a reporter for the *New York Herald* observed that "nearly all the butchers, vegetable dealers, hucksters, dealers in fish, fruit, flowers, pork [and] poultry," were slaves, "some of them of the pure African type." An editor for the *Nashville Union* was transfixed watching an all-black street funeral, "followed by about one hundred negroes, walking along the pavement, two abreast." The editor added: "Our Northern friends say that neither dead nor live ones receive so much respectful attention in the free states."[25]

Members of the large New York delegation, which included the scandal-prone and headline-making Fernando Wood, Mayor of New York City, crammed into the large Mills House, which was also the official headquarters for the Douglas campaign, with more than 130 cots packed into a single meeting room on the hotel's second floor. The Jefferson Davis-friendly Alabama and North Carolina delegations holed up at the nearby Charleston Hotel, along with the Johnson men of Tennessee, where more than 500 barrels of lager beer and domestic liquors were in supply.

The convention itself would be held at the South Carolina Institute, described by the enterprising journalist Murat Halstead as a place filled with "old-fashioned, wooden-bottomed chairs" and "gaudy and uncouth ornamentation around the hall." Located off a cobblestone street, the hall was a noisy place, so noisy that convention officials quickly decided to order the dumping of loads of hay on the street in an attempt to soften the sound of the endless wagons clomping by.[26]

But this was a convention and noise was just a natural part of the proceedings: every morning party officials threw out free tickets to the day's proceedings from the windows of the hall, causing a frantic and loud dash among outsiders hoping to be insiders. Some 65 reporters, watching the mayhem, tried to do their work inside a series of steamy, over-crowded rooms, sending their dispatches over a wire running from Charleston to Richmond and beyond.[27]

Reporters who had followed the House balloting for John Sherman could recognize in Charleston several prominent players from the Speakership contest: John Clark of Missouri, the man who had done so much to damage Sherman by connecting him with Hinton Helper's *Impending Crisis of the South;* John McClernand of Illinois, who had for a while run against Sherman and was now lobbying for Douglas; and Thomas Bocock of Virginia, also a one-time Sherman challenger, currently backing fellow Virginian Hunter.

Caleb Cushing arrived by steamship from Baltimore on Saturday, April 21, after an earlier cruise from Boston made pleasant by the presence of a band and choice liquors. On the opening day of the convention, members of the Committee on Permanent Organization selected Cushing as the conclave's presiding president. It was a curious choice given that Cushing was known to favor Pierce, Davis or Guthrie, in that order, for the nomination. He was also generally antagonistic towards Douglas.

But Cushing, forceful with what reporter Halstead described as a "clear, musical and powerful" voice, was also a skilled parliamentarian well regarded for being both patient and fair. He would need both virtues in abundance in the days ahead.[28]

"In a great deliberative assembly like this, it is not the presiding officer in whom the strength resides," Cushing diplomatically told the delegates as he took possession of the gavel. "It is not his strength, but *yours*—your intelligence, your sense of order, your instinct of self-respect."

Niceties out of the way, Cushing launched into a vigorous pro-Union speech that seemed to attack both abolitionists in the North and slaveholders in the South, any group boasting secession. Such thinking, proclaimed Cushing, represented a "stupid and half insane spirit of faction and fanatacism" designed to "hurry our land to revolution and to civil war."

Proponents of secession, Cushing continued, were in reality "the branded enemies of the Constitution." And it was up to the good Democrats assembled, he added, to defeat them.

"In the name of our dear country, with the help of God, we will do it," Cushing declared to another loud round of applause from the delegates, some of whom from the Southern states just enjoyed hearing a good speech, no matter what the point of view.[29]

As Cushing took control, the convention was confronted with undoubtedly its most important challenge—not who the nominee would be, but what platform he would run on. Southerners were inspired by the resolutions presented in February by Davis. The Democratic party, said Davis man William Yancey of Alabama, should commit itself squarely to Constitutional principles, meaning that neither Congress nor a territorial legislature had the power to abolish slavery, and even more, that Congress was obliged to defend the rights of anyone bringing a slave into a new territory.

"Ours is the property invaded," proclaimed Yancey in an address that captivated the convention. "Ours are the institutions which are at stake; ours is the peace that is to be destroyed; our is the property that is to be destroyed; our is the honor at stake—the honor of children, the honor of families, the lives, perhaps, of all."[30]

In response George Pugh of Ohio, a Douglas man, saw no reason for the convention to be so particular about things, contending that the party platform of 1856, which committed itself to state's rights but did not specifically defend slavery in the Yancey manner, was enough. Yet he prompted outrage when he also said that as a Northern Democrat he was offended that Southerners thought they could dictate the party platform, with the Northerners meekly signing off on a document expressly condoning slavery. "Gentlemen of the South, you mistake us. You mistake us," Pugh declared as his speech reached a rhetorical high. "We will not do it."[31]

When Pugh's view prevailed on Monday, April 30, an alarmingly large number of Southern delegates declared their intention of withdrawing from the convention. Alabama delegate Leroy Walker of Alabama handed a letter to Cushing noting that because the convention had failed to commit itself to protecting the rights of a slave-owner to the "enjoyment of his property in the territories," the Alabama delegation would return home. This dramatic declaration was followed by similar statements of exit from the Florida, Mississippi and Texas delegations.[32]

The evening of that same day the dissident Southerners met for a street rally. Yancey, with a lifelong love for the dramatic gesture, declared the beginning of a new party dedicated to what he described as "constitutional Democratic principles." This party would put forth its own nominee for president. Under the moonlight, the loud rally was an upbeat declaration of principle, the first volley in a war of Southern liberation. "The pen of the historian," predicted Yancey, relishing the moment, "was nibbed to write the story of a new revolution."[33]

Initially the Douglas men were not certain that the Southern exit was such a bad thing, particularly after most of the Georgia and Virginia delegations issued statements vowing to stick with the convention.

The Southern exit, in fact, might have made things significantly easier for the Douglas men by getting rid of the delegates most likely to vote for Davis, Guthrie, Hunter or even

Johnson. A correspondent for the *New York Tribune* accurately reckoned that if Douglas was to now be nominated at all he would "almost certainly be nominated by Northern votes," which included the big New York delegation.[34]

But then Cushing single-handedly destroyed the dreams of the Douglas men by announcing that no one could be nominated without first winning two-thirds of the delegates who had been *sent* to the convention, not two-thirds of those who still remained. This was a death blow to the Douglas campaign as it meant having to get 202 votes for a candidate who, at best, was certain of only 150.

"While it is impossible that Mr. Douglas under the new rule can be nominated," candidly observed the *Charleston Mercury*, "the difficulty of making any nomination is increased." Delegates shortly began to wonder who might benefit the most from Cushing's ruling, imagining a sudden surge for Guthrie or Hunter, while others thought a good ticket might be Davis for president and New York's Fernando Wood for vice-president. "Everything is in confusion and excitement here," a reporter for the *Baltimore American* telegraphed on May 2 from Charleston.[35]

When the delegates began to vote on the nomination later that same day, the worst fears of the Douglas men were quickly realized. In an endless series of ballots the total for Douglas was never greater than 151 votes. Guthrie emerged as a reliable second, getting as many as 66 votes on the 40th ballot. Davis refused to let his name be entered into contention.[36]

The balloting went on throughout the oppressively hot day and into the late evening. The Douglas men lobbied delegates pledged to both Guthrie and Hunter, asking them to give the "Little Giant" a chance and pointing out that, despite the

Southern opposition to him, Douglas was not only the only candidate who had any reasonable expectation of winning the nomination, but was probably also the only Democrat in November who could beat either Seward or the still-relatively unknown Lincoln.

Surely those who were opposed to "Little Giant" did not want to destroy the Democratic party's best chances in 1860, the Douglas men asked. After 57 ballots, the answer was not promising.

The fact that the vote total for Douglas remained static prompted Guthrie's supporters to think that their man might have a real chance for victory after all: "It is ascertained that most of the seceding delegates are willing to take Guthrie if he is nominated by the regular convention," the *New York Tribune* reported, detecting a movement both inside and outside the convention in favor of the Kentuckian. When the Johnson men, after consulting with their candidate but getting no direction, decided to throw their support Guthrie's way, things only looked better.[37]

Prospects for Douglas, meanwhile, suffered a blow when the New York delegation threatened to withdraw its unenthusiastic support for him if he did not go over the top by the 60th ballot. This immediately changed the entire picture for Douglas, and rather than risk the outright defeat of their candidate, the Douglas team decided the next day to call for an adjournment of the convention. Cushing, for once, was cooperative. On the motion of Charles Russell of Virginia, the delegates voted 195 to 55 to meet again in Baltimore on June 18.

The Charleston convention was now suddenly over, with the fortunes of Douglas and the Democratic party dashed in the process.

As the delegates readied to leave Charleston, Cushing, wishing out loud, reminded them that they had only ended a convention, not a great national union. "We have held our way manfully on until we have come to be a great Republic," he said of a Union that had always included a Northern and Southern section. "Shall we cease to be such? I will not believe it."[38]

In the immediate aftermath of the disaster at Charleston, journalists thought that the Douglas men had probably saved themselves by ending things as swiftly as they did. The *Charleston Courier* described the decision as a "master stroke of policy."[39]

But the truth was that the Democrats in general were greatly depressed. Robert Johnson, the son of Andrew Johnson, who had the additional unpleasant duty of trying to keep his brother Charles from drinking on the trip back to Tennessee (a task that proved impossible), thought that the convention in Charleston had been a "general row, and injured the Democratic party more than anything that has happened to it for years."[40]

Albert Graham, a loyal Democratic editor in Tennessee, suggested that unless the Democrats made things right in Baltimore, the "permanency of the party as a national organization is rather doubtful."[41]

From his Sherwood Forest estate, ex-president Tyler frankly wrote to his friend John Cunningham: "The severance which took place at Charleston filled me with apprehension and regret." President Buchanan, greatly dreading the idea that Douglas might still somehow prevail, frankly told Robert Tyler: "Everything looks bad, not just for the party, but for the country."[42]

Republicans very obviously had a different take on things. The pro-Lincoln *Chicago Tribune* declared that the "conflict at Charleston" symbolized a general hopelessness within the party because the differences between Democrats in a state like Illinois and Democrats in a state like Alabama "are radical and irrepressible." William Robinson, a columnist for the *Springfield Daily Republican*, agreed: "They are irretrievably split to pieces. They have no principles in common. And they hate each other, as men, with invincible hatred."[43]

In Washington, Josiah Lucas, postmaster in the House of Representatives, studied the faces of the Democrats as they returned from Charleston and observed: "I never looked upon such despondency. Despair absolutely reigns supreme."

Writing to Lincoln on May 6, Lucas added that he had recently observed Douglas in the Senate chamber with his feet kicked up on a desk, casually smoking a cigar: "He assumed an air of careless indifference, yet to one who knows him well, his attempt to wear a placid brow but made the attempt at deception more apparent."

"The 'Giant,'" Lucas noted with delight, "is evidently in a bad fix."[44]

CHAPTER TWO ENDNOTES

[1]"Personal," *New York Tribune*, 8 February 1860, p. 6.

[2]*Congressional Globe*, 58-59.

[3]Lynda Laswell Crist, *The Papers of Jefferson Davis, Volume 6-1856-1860* (Baton Rouge: Louisiana State University Press, 1989), 276-77.

[4]"Correspondence of the Mercury," *Charleston Mercury*, 16 January 1860, p. 1.

[5]"The Douglas State Convention," *Chicago Tribune*, 6 January 1860, p. 2; Douglas and the Presidency," *New York Tribune*, 2 March 1860, p. 6.

[6]Robert W. Johannsen, *Stephen A. Douglas* (New York: Oxford University Press, 1973), 725.

[7]*Congressional Globe*, 542.

[8]Johanssen, *Stephen A. Douglas*, 585.

[9]Franklin Pierce to George Strong, 17 February 1860, Franklin Pierce Papers, Series 3, Reel 6.

[10]Henry Wax to Andrew Johnson, 13 February 1860, Andrew Johnson Papers, Series 2, Reel 39.

[11]Anthony Ten Eyck to Andrew Johnson, 20 February 1860, Andrew Johnson Papers, Series 2, Reel 39.

[12]*Congressional Globe*, 997-98; "News from Washington," *New York Herald*, 9 March 1860, p. 4.

[13]"Washington Social Life," *Springfield Daily Republican*, 21 February 1860, p. 2; "Presidential Dinner," *Charleston Mercury*, 13 April 1860, p. 2.

[14]John Bassett Moore, *The Works of James Buchanan, Volume X, 1865-1860* (New York: Antiquarian Press, 1960), 399-405; Arthur Schlesinger, Jr., *Congress Investigates—A Documented History, 1792-1974* (New York: Chelsea House Publishers, 1975), 1105-09.

[15]Schlesinger, *Congress Investigates*, 1115-16.

[16]Leroy P. Graf, *The Papers of Andrew Johnson, Volume 3, 1858-1860* (Knoxville: University of Tennessee Press, 1972), 631, 641.

[17]Frank Blair to Martin Van Buren, 13 February 1860, Martin Van Buren Papers, Reel 34, Series 2.

[18]James Buchanan to Robert Tyler, 21 February 1860, John Tyler Papers, Reel 2, Series 1.

[19]*Congressional Globe*, 1436.

[20]"The Charleston Convention," *New York Herald*, 11 March 1860, p. 5.

[21]"The Democratic Convention and the South Carolina Institute," *Charleston Courier*, 9 April 1860, p. 4.

[22]"National Democratic Committee," *Charleston Courier*, 9 April 1860, p. 4.

[23]"The Banquet," *New York Herald*, 16 April 1860, p. 4.

[24]"Travel to Charleston By Sea," *New York Herald*, 12 April 1860, p. 6; "Charleston Convention," *New York Times*, 23 April 1860, p. 1; "Convention Correspondence," *Charleston Courier*, 8 May 1860, p. 1.

[25]"Our Convention Correspondence," *New York Herald*, 26 April 1860, p. 3;

"Convention Correspondence," *Charleston Courier*, 28 April 1860, p. 1.

[26]William B. Hesseltine, *Three Against Lincoln—Murat Halstead Reports the Caucuses of 1860* (Baton Rouge: Louisiana State University Press, 1960), 7.

[27]"A Scene," *Charleston Mercury*, 26 April 1860, p. 2; "The Press," *Charleston Mercury*, 26 April 1860, p. 2; "The Charleston Convention," *Baltimore American*, 23 April 1860, p. 1.

[28]Hesseltine, *Three Against Lincoln*, 27-28.

[29]"News of the Day," *New York Times,* 25 April 129. p. 4, col. 1; *Official Proceedings of the Democratic National Convention Held in 1860* (Cleveland: Nevins Print, 1860), 16-17.

[30]*Official Proceedings,* 37-39.

[31]Ibid.

[32]"From Charleston," *Springfield Daily Republican,* 28 April 1860, p. 4; "Charleston Convention," *New York Times,* 27 April 1860, p. 1; "The Charleston Convention," *New York Herald,* 1 May 1860, p. 5.

[33] Bruce Catton, *The Coming Fury,* New York: Doubleday & Company, 1961), 36.

[34]"The Charleston Convention," *New York Tribune,* 3 May 1860, p. 5.

[35]"The Convention," *Charleston Mercury,* 2 May 1860, p. 1; "Charleston Convention," *Baltimore American,* 3 May 1860, p. 1.

[36]*Official Proceedings,* 74-88.

[37]"The Charleston Convention," *New York Tribune,* 4 May 1860, p. 5.

[38]*Official Proceedings,* 90-91.

[39]"Correspondence of the Courier," *Charleston Courier,* 7 May 1860, p. 4.

[40]Robert Johnson to Andrew Johnson, 8 May 1860, Andrew Johnson Papers, Series 2, Reel 39.

[41]Albert Graham to Andrew Johnson, 23 May 1860, Andrew Johnson Papers, Series 2, Reel 39.

[42]Buchanan in his February 21st letter to Robert Tyler predicted that the Democrats of the North "will find themselves outwitted there [in Charleston]. The inertia of 15 states all of one mind will battle evil." Lyon G. Tyler, *The Letters and Times of the Tylers—Volume II* (New York: DaCapo Press, 1970), 558; James Buchanan to Robert Tyler, 21 February 1860, John Tyler Papers, Reel 2, Series 1.

[43]"The Seceeders at Charleston," *Chicago Tribune*, 2 May 1860, p. 2; "From Boston," *Springfield Daily Republican*, 4 May 1860, p. 2.

[44]Josiah Lucas to Abraham Lincoln, 6 May 1860, Abraham Lincoln Papers, Reel 6.

CHAPTER THREE

"Nothing Will Stop Us But Old Fogy Politicians"

Abraham Lincoln, closely following events in Charleston, may have enjoyed reading about the implosion of the convention, but not for a moment did he imagine that Stephen Douglas would not be the eventual Democratic nominee with a strong chance of winning the White House.

It was a sentiment shared by certain of Lincoln's supporters, including Herman Kreisman, a German-American political activist, who told Lincoln that if Douglas did become the Democratic nominee "We may as well hang up our fiddle first as last—particularly we in Illinois."[1]

Lincoln, acknowledging the pivotal importance of Illinois in the 1860 race, agreed, offering a swipe to his rivals for the Republican nomination, Judge Edward Bates of Missouri and

William Seward, in the process. "I think neither Seward nor Bates can carry Illinois if Douglas shall be on the track," Lincoln confided to Lyman Trumbull, "and that either of them can, if he shall not be."[2]

Such configurations taxed the imagination of politicians throughout the spring of 1860 and worked in many directions: Albert Clapp, a Seward supporter in Buffalo, frankly told his candidate: "I fear the nomination of Douglas, for it will make our own road to success more dusty & difficult."[3]

But Democratic editor Albert Graham perceived a synergy between Lincoln and Douglas, telling Andrew Johnson that because Lincoln as the Republican nominee would likely do well in such states as Illinois, Douglas would be the "only champion who can successfully cope with him [Lincoln] in the northern states."[4]

In a way that few observers appreciated at the time, Graham understood that Lincoln and Douglas needed each other.

The collapse of the Charleston convention, however, inevitably changed the calculations of many Republicans. Seward, always an optimist, actually thought his chances had significantly improved based on the theory that if the Democrats didn't nominate someone from the Midwest, the Republicans wouldn't either, freeing themselves to run with a New Yorker named Seward.

Seward had good reason to dream: Lining up support in Minnesota, Wisconsin, California and Michigan, which he would add to the massive 70 votes that New York would cast at the Republican convention, Seward by March and April was undoubtedly the front-runner. He was "the strongest man in the nation," said a letter-writer from Connecticut to the

taller pilings in order to make way for a new sewer system, and a two-mile tunnel that would be dug some 3,400 feet under Lake Michigan to bring fresh water to the city.

Securing Chicago as the host city for the Republican convention was a signal achievement for the Lincoln forces. In December of 1859 members of the Republican National Committee, meeting in New York, mulled over the presentations of city leaders from Buffalo, Cincinnati, Cleveland, Harrisburg, Indianapolis and St. Louis before hearing from Norman Judd, chairman of the Illinois State Central Committee, who suggested Chicago as a "good neutral ground where everyone would have an even chance."[16]

Because the committee members did not regard Lincoln as a major contender, they agreed with Judd, who took the additional step of talking local railroad companies into lowering their rates during the week of the convention, allowing thousands of Lincoln fans, primarily from the southern part of Illinois, to flood into the city, talking him up and cheering his name, all of which undoubtedly impressed both the uncommitted and wavering delegates from other states.[17]

Chicago leaders also enthusiastically got behind the construction of a massive wood-framed building at the corner of First and Market streets which was quickly dubbed the "Wigwam" because "the chiefs of the Republican party were to meet there."[18]

Built in just over a month at a cost of less than $7,000 (which was underwritten by the Chicago Republican Club), the Wigwam was designed to accommodate up to 10,000 people. It had an interior of rough wood, a series of massive pillars supporting a gallery that flowed around three sides of the building, and a vast stage with space enough for at least

600 people. The *Chicago Tribune*, which had enthusiastically supported the project from inception, could hardly contain its excitement as the Wigwam neared completion, noting that once the thousands of delegates from other states entered the structure and realized how quickly it had all been put together, it would speak powerfully to "the way things are done" in Chicago.[19]

And the way things were done in Chicago also included making certain there was plenty of hotel space at reasonable rates, restaurants near the Wigwam operating into the evening, and train service, always train service, from anywhere to anywhere, throughout the day for the delegates. It was all designed to show that this was a city that indeed got things done, usually in a hurry, even when it came to nominating a president.

But while all of these factors undoubtedly created a more amenable environment in Chicago for a Lincoln victory, it was the candidate himself who, beginning in early 1860, formulated a plan to make that victory certain.

Lincoln accepted as the presidential year dawned that he was not well known. This he saw as a good thing. In fact, up to 1858, he was a virtual unknown: heading up a medium-sized law practice in Springfield, Lincoln served for 8 years in the state legislature and one term in the U.S. House of Representatives from 1847 to 1849, before running for the U.S. Senate in 1854 and losing.

But 1854 was the year that saw the passage of the Kansas-Nebraska Act, an act that transformed Lincoln into a man with a cause, convinced that the idea of even considering extending slavery into the western territories meant that eventually the country was going to have to address the larger question of being a nation that allowed slavery to flourish or prohibited it altogether.

He enthusiastically supported the creation of the Republican party in Illinois in 1856, and at the age of 47 was just a little bit older than the young John Sherman Republicans who were running and getting elected to Congress across the country that year. The fact that his fellow state Republicans tried to run him for the vice-presidency in 1856 showed that he was genuinely well-liked within Illinois party circles, so much so that his nomination for the U.S. Senate in 1858 against Stephen Douglas, who was running for re-election, ended up being a foregone conclusion.

In accepting that nomination, Lincoln displayed his remarkable powers of argument, borrowing the Biblical phrase, "A house divided against itself cannot stand."

"We are now far into the fifth year since a policy was initiated with the avowed object and confident purpose of putting an end to slavery agitation," Lincoln remarked. "Under the operation of that policy, that agitation has not only not ceased, but has constantly augmented. In my opinion, it will not cease until a crisis shall have been reached and passed. 'A house divided against itself cannot stand.' I believe this government cannot endure permanently half slave and half free. I do not expect the Union to be dissolved; I do not expect the house to fall; but I do expect it will cease to be divided. It will become all one thing, or all the other."[20]

Lincoln's words provided only a hint of what was to come: a series of seven debates across the state with incumbent Douglas that turned out to be the political sensation of the year. Although Lincoln would win the popular vote, he would fail against Douglas in the state legislature where U.S. Senate elections were ultimately decided. But he emerged from the contest as a national curiosity, honoring invitations in 1859 to speak in Iowa, Wisconsin, Indiana and Ohio where he made new friends who wondered if the Republicans could do worse than nominate this tall and strangely calm man from the flat prairie lands of Illinois.

By early 1860, Lincoln was regarded among national party leaders as, at best, a possible vice-presidential running mate for Seward. But smaller newspapers across the country were beginning to imagine bigger things, the *Chester County Times* in Pennsylvania being fairly typical when it declared in February: "There is no one who has a firmer hold on the confidence and affections of the people of the Great West, or is more an object of their enthusiastic admiration, than Abraham Lincoln."[21]

Lincoln substantially enhanced his national fortunes in February when he agreed to accept an invitation to speak at the Plymouth Church in Brooklyn. By the time he arrived in New York, the event had been moved to the Cooper Union in Manhattan. It was, for Lincoln, a lucky switch: the Cooper Union was a popular hall that regularly headlined the great thinkers and speakers of the day. The simple fact that Lincoln would now appear in such surroundings undoubtedly added to the interest that many New Yorkers already had in him, an interest that was in no way diminished by a heavy snow storm. Introduced by William Cullen Bryant, the editor of the *New York Evening Post*, who enjoyed reminding his listeners that Lincoln had received the most popular votes in his run for the Senate in 1858, while Douglas secured only a "legislative appointment," Lincoln, somewhat tentatively at first, told his listeners that slavery had become virtually the only issue in the 1860 campaign.[22]

Gently nudging his audience towards his driving theory that the nation must eventually address the question of allowing slavery to exist *anywhere*, Lincoln said of the Southern slaveholders: "All they ask we could readily grant if we thought slavery right. All we ask, they could as readily grant, if they thought it wrong. Their thinking it right, and our thinking it wrong, is the precise fact upon which depends the whole controversy. Thinking it right, as they do, they are not to blame for desiring its full recognition, as being right. But thinking it wrong, as we do, can we yield to them? Can we cast our votes with their view and against our own?"

Recognizing that Lincoln was presenting matters in a rationalistic manner rarely employed by fiery abolitionist speakers, the Cooper Union audience rose to its feel almost as one as he concluded: "Let us have faith that right makes might. And in that faith, let us to the end dare to do our duty as we understand it."[23]

Lincoln's address won him high praise from the New York press, in particular the *New York Tribune*, which described it as "one of the happiest and most convincing arguments ever made in this city." The paper added: "No man ever before made such an impression on his first appeal to a New York audience."[24]

But New York and most of the East coast was still Seward territory. If Lincoln had simply returned to Illinois after his Cooper Union appearance, it is likely that the political impact of his trip would not have been as great. Instead he accepted invitations to speak throughout New England over the course of the next two weeks, appearing at packed halls everywhere and in every case leaving behind impressed Republicans who began to see him as a compelling alternative to Seward. "He is never offensive and steals away willingly into his train of belief persons who were opposed to him," noted the *Manchester Mirror* after Lincoln spoke in New Hampshire.[25]

As word spread of Lincoln's talks, more invitations reached him. Isaac Pomeroy, a businessman and member of the Young Men's Working Club of the Republican Party in New Jersey, asked Lincoln to continue what he described as his "patriotic work" with a speech in Newark; Leon Smith, the chairman of a local party committee in Portland, wanted him to come to Maine; attorney Alexander Henry hoped Lincoln might stop off in Buffalo to deliver a few comments on his way back to Illinois.[26]

Lincoln tried to keep up with his correspondence, politely declining invitations he could not fulfill. It was not until March 14, for example, when he was back in Springfield, that he was able to respond to Harvey, explaining that the invitations he had accepted after his Cooper Union appearance "carried me so far beyond my allotted time that I could not consistently add another."[27]

But as trying as it had been, Lincoln's trip created a reservoir of good will among the people who had heard him speak. Typical was the comment of editor James Babcock in Connecticut who told Lincoln on April 8: "We here remember your speech with great satisfaction...I have heard your name mentioned more freely than ever in connection with the Chicago nomination, and by some who have had other views or whose feelings were previously committed in favor of another of the distinguished members of the Republican party."[28]

Yet still the odds were daunting: Ira Buck, an Illinois businessman, told Lincoln of a "large delegation of members of Congress" making plans to attend the Chicago convention (the most prominent Congressional Republicans, John Sherman, Schuyler Colfax and Speaker Pennington, would stay behind while the House remained in session). But whether they remained in Washington or went to Chicago, most of the Republican leaders, thought Buck, had already revealed their feelings about the nomination, adding: "I think Mr. Seward is the prominent man and a large majority of the members are for him."[29]

Despite such reports, Lincoln by April had organized a multi-layered command structure, partly made up of some of his closest friends, that would fan out inside the Wigwam making contact with every potential supporter. The team included Norman Judd; the portly circuit court judge David Davis; state auditor Jesse Dubois; and Mark Delahay of Kansas (who borrowed money from Lincoln to get to Chicago). Outside the immediate structure, but still willing to work for Lincoln and—like almost everyone else—offering him unsolicited advice, was Nathan Knapp, a delegate from Scott County, and William Butler, an old Springfield friend.

That Lincoln kept tight control of his team from Springfield was seen in a quick dispatch he sent to Delahay several days before the official opening of the convention: "Look to Minnesota and Iowa," he instructed, before warning that Delahay should be "careful to give no offense, and keep cool under all circumstances."[30]

As the women of the convention's decoration committee hurriedly put the final touches on the Wigwam, which included tacking wreathes of evergreens to the stage and pillars, reporters noted that Seward's early delegate lead—thought to be at least 170 of the 233 needed for nomination—remained firm. Ohio Governor Salmon Chase had at least 46 votes from his state, while Bates had the 18 delegates of Missouri along with scattered support elsewhere for a total of 40 to 50 delegates.

"Mr. Seward will lead, Mr. Bates will come next, and Mr. Chase will be third having some New England votes," the *New York Tribune* predicted on May 14, noting almost in a postscript that Lincoln is "much pressed by the Illinois delegation as a compromise candidate."[31]

An air of manic energy, so unlike the gloom of the Democratic meeting in Charleston, was predominant in Chicago. Murat Halstead, writing for the *Cincinnati Commercial,* saw it on the afternoon of the first day of the convention as he watched officials open the front doors of the hall. "Three torrents of men roared in, rushing headlong for front positions. The standing room, holding 4,500 people, was packed in about five minutes. The galleries, where only gentleman accompanied by ladies are admitted, and which contain nearly 3,000 persons, was already full."[32]

A reporter for the *Indianapolis Journal* noticed the same moving pool of humanity and remarked: "There was no way to get along but to stand still and let the slowly drifting mass move you as a glacier does gravel stones."[33]

The excitement indicated a growing confidence among the Republicans that this year was their year, the year that would see the election of the first Republican president in history. As such, there was also a prevailing disposition to get things done quickly and cleanly. On the first day it was decided that a simple majority of the delegates present would be enough for anyone to be nominated, the two-thirds requirement that proved so deadly for the Democrats in Charleston being swiftly rejected.

The Republicans also efficiently settled on a platform prohibiting slavery in all of the territories and condemning the

African slave trade, which it called a "crime against humanity and a burning shame to our country and age."[34]

Trying to harness the excitement of the delegates for his candidate, Weed and his fellow New Yorkers staged a loud and colorful parade for Seward on the streets of Chicago that got a lot of good-willed attention from the much more numerous Lincoln devotees. Meanwhile, Seward, waiting at his Auburn, New York mansion for word of his nomination, received a stream of telegraphs chronicling the initial confidence of his team in Chicago. "There is a large lobby of interested croakers," New York Congressman Elbridge Spaulding said on May 15 of the delegates who seemed willing to make a deal for any candidate, "but we feel confident of a favorable result."[35]

The following day, Spaulding reported: "There is more opposition by the friends of other candidates than we anticipated, but we are still confident of success."[36]

The day after that, as delegates neared the momentous presidential balloting, Spaulding refused to believe in anything but the eventual success of his candidate, wiring Seward: "Your friends are firm & confident that you will be nominated after a few ballots."[37]

But reporters, repeatedly interviewing delegates from crucial Pennsylvania and Ohio, noticed a trend: While the "confidence of the Seward party is firmer than ever," observed the *New York Tribune* on May 15, Lincoln "seems to be gaining ground."[38]

That was certainly the view of the Lincoln men as they sent to the candidate quick updates on the situation. "Your chances are brightening," Butler reported on May 14. "Illinois, Indiana, Iowa, Maine & New Hampshire will present a solid front for you." On the same day, Delahay concluded: "The stock is gradually rising. Indiana is all right. Ohio is prepared to do a good post after Chase has had his compliments paid him. New Hampshire and a part of N Jersey are talking out for you."[39]

The next day, Davis and Dubois jointly signed a telegram to Lincoln displaying a young confidence that seemed to symbolize the young party itself: "Nothing will stop us but old fogy politicians. The heart of the delegates are with us." As the actual voting began on May 18, Lincoln received another dispatch, unsigned but most likely from Davis, remarking: "The name of Lincoln is proposed with deafening cheers, much louder than Seward's or any other mentioned."[40]

Although delegates clamored to begin the presidential balloting on the evening of May 17, tally papers were not yet ready, prompting the convention to adjourn until the next morning. The delay was fine with the Lincoln team, which put the additional hours to good use by trying to win over additional wavering delegates. Even so, the reach and power of the New Yorkers seemed daunting. Delahay told Lincoln he was certain the Seward men were spreading offers of patronage and wondered if Lincoln should do the same. "I know that you have no relish for such a game," Delahay added.[41]

In fact, Lincoln refused to bargain with anyone, writing back in Springfield a message on the margins of the *Missouri Democrat* newspaper, which was shortly delivered to Davis: "Make no contracts that will bind me."[42]

When voting at last began the results of Lincoln's New England forays was instantly seen as he won 7 of New Hampshire's 10 delegate votes. Maine, where Republicans heard of his successful speeches, gave him 6 of its 10 votes. The early balloting made the Lincoln men hopeful until big

New York cast all 70 of its votes for Seward. The Lincoln team knew this was coming, but even so the effect was galvanizing as Seward shot to a strong lead and the loud New Yorkers got even louder. Meanwhile a reporter for the *Indianapolis Journal* noticed that every time the convention secretary read out the results of each state's ballot, he yelled up to the Wigwam's open roof ventilator where a man heard the results and yelled the news to another man standing on the edge of the building. That man then "shouted it to the crowd outside and thus gave instant information of every vote to the whole 30,000 congregated there."[43]

Lincoln won unanimous votes out of Indiana and Illinois, giving him 48 more delegates. But the Pennsylvania delegation, frequently openly arguing on the convention floor, gave 47 and a half votes to home state favorite U.S. Senator Simon Cameron. Ohio stuck with Chase, giving him 34 votes— although Lincoln managed to get 8.

By the end of the first ballot delegates were surprised to see that although Seward's total at 173 and a half was big, it wasn't overwhelming. Meanwhile Lincoln had done what two days earlier would have seemed impossible, coming in second with 102 votes. No one else was close. "The first ballot clearly indicated Mr. Seward's defeat," the *New York Tribune* later concluded.[44]

Delegates readied for an immediate second ballot which started out badly for Seward when Lincoln picked up additional votes in New Hampshire, Vermont, Rhode Island and Connecticut before the chaotic Pennsylvania delegation finally weighed in with a shocker, abandoning Cameron and swinging 48 votes to Lincoln. The effect was electric as the convention erupted in roars of approval.

Ohio continued to give most of its vote to Chase, but even here Lincoln gained 6 more delegates. The 2nd ballot result: 184 and a half for Seward, 181 for Lincoln. "As the first ballot developed itself, the New York delegation looked like a funeral procession," a reporter for the *New York Herald* noted with obvious delight, "and the second ballot intensified their somber appearance."[45]

Ballot number three showed excited shifts to Lincoln everywhere, enough for him to end up with 231 and a half votes—just one and a half votes shy of the nomination. In what reporter Halstead called "ten ticks of a watch," delegate David Cartter of Ohio stood up to announce, as he put it, "the change of four votes of Ohio from Mr. Chase to Mr. Lincoln."[46]

That was it—Lincoln had won and the response both in and out of the Wigwam was riotous: "It was absolutely as if a burst of thunder had broken over the house, bellowing sometimes in awful concert and sometimes in roaring fragments," said the *Indianapolis Journal* reporter, "and at the same instant the crowd outside began to shout and yell, not in 'hurrahs,' but continuous screaming, as if they couldn't afford to stop long enough to break the sound into words."[47]

As the pandemonium increased, the New Yorkers sat in an oasis of silence. Weed covered his head with his hands. Their despair was made even worse with the knowledge that Greeley of the *New York Tribune*, who should have been one of them, had instead gone from delegation to delegation speaking against Seward, satisfying an old grudge while also expressing his genuine conviction that Seward would lose the fall elections.

The defeat of Seward went down hard with many who remembered his eloquent anti-slavery speeches and early efforts to create a Republican party in New York. "Let those who nominated Lincoln, elect him. We are against him here," Gilbert Davidson, a Seward man in Albany, angrily wired to the defeated candidate. Another New Yorker and long-time friend, Lewis Benedict, remarked: "All our house mourns over the result of the Chicago convention," adding "I am intensely, utterly disgusted."[48]

From Boston, supporter Arthur Dexter told Seward that Lincoln's nomination was a cause of "much regret to us here in Massachusetts," while Charles Sumner, the famed abolitionist Senator from Massachusetts, consoled Seward: "My personal feelings have been so much disturbed by the result at Chicago that I cannot yet appreciate it as a public act."[49]

"Many turned against him with a sorrowing feeling," concluded a columnist for the *Springfield Daily Republican* of Seward's defeat. But in an attempt to ensure unity, William Evarts, the chairman of the New York delegation, briefly brought the convention back to order when he paid tribute to Seward as a man from whom "most of us learned to love Republican principles and the Republican party." Evarts then moved to make Lincoln's nomination unanimous. In a symbolic nod to the Eastern wing of the party, the delegates named Hannibal Hamlin, U.S. Senator from Maine and a Seward man, as Lincoln's running mate.[50]

In Springfield, J. B. Pierce, an operator for the Illinois and Mississippi Telegraph Company, sent Lincoln the first word of his nomination and then realizing the historic moment, kept a copy of the message himself, later telling Lincoln it was the "first intelligence you received announcing your nomination for President at the Chicago Convention."[51]

That message was quickly followed by a series of others from the members of the Lincoln team congratulating the successful candidate, but warning him not to come to Chicago to receive the nomination in person. Instead, Lincoln was told by George Ashmun, convention chairman, that a committee would arrive the following afternoon in Springfield to "inform you officially of your nomination for the President of the United States."[52]

As Lincoln waited for that visit and wrote and re-wrote a brief acceptance address, he received messages from supporters around the country overjoyed by his victory. In Washington, Trumbull, who had three weeks earlier predicted that Lincoln could not beat Seward, now remarked: "We heard your nomination at 3 o'clock this afternoon & our friends are greatly rejoiced." Schuyler Colfax, who had backed Bates for the nomination, was quick-thinking enough to joke: "I need not say how heartily I join with your *original* friends in their greetings to you." From Connecticut, publisher James Babcock told Lincoln that his nomination gave "courage, hope and confidence to our friends, some of whom feared an injurious selection."[53]

But the good feeling engendered by Lincoln's nomination was hardly universal. Democrats, happy to be rid of Seward, suddenly contemplated this new, strange presence from Illinois.

In Hartford, Connecticut, former Governor Thomas Hart Seymour was troubled. Writing to Franklin Pierce one day after Lincoln's nomination, Seymour reported that "They [the Republicans] get rid of the axiom which attaches itself to Seward without giving up Seward's views."

Continued Seymour: "We ought to beat them, but mischief rules the hour and no one can tell what is to be *our* picture."[54]

CHAPTER THREE ENDNOTES

[1] Herman Kreisman to Abraham Lincoln, 11 April 1860, Abraham Lincoln Papers, Reel 6.

[2] Roy P. Basler, *The Collected Works of Abraham Lincoln, Volume IV* (New Brunswick, New Jersey: Rutgers University Press, 1953), 45-46.

[3] Almon Clapp to William Seward, 23 April 1860, Papers of William H. Seward, Reel 59.

[4] Albert Graham to Andrew Johnson, 23 May 1860, Andrew Johnson Papers, Series 2, Reel 39.

[5] "The Presidency," *New York Tribune*, 17 March 1860, p. 10.

[6] Lyman Trumbull to Abraham Lincoln, 24 April 1860, Abraham Lincoln Papers, Reel 6.

[7] "Chicago Convention—The Nominee," *Chicago Tribune*, 10 March 1860, p. 2; Carl Sandburg, *Abraham Lincoln—The Prairie Years and The War Years* (San Diego: A Harvest Book, 1982), 165.

[8] "Mr. Seward a Hero," *Charleston Mercury*, 10 January 1860, p. 1; Fabius Finch to Abraham Lincoln, 16 April 1860, Abraham Lincoln Papers, Reel 6.

[9] Ten years later, the "higher law" reference still resonated with Seward's supporters. William Burgett, a Seward man in Westmoreland, New York, told the Senator on February 20 that anyone who believed in the concept of a higher law would almost naturally be "both humane and just to the South as well as to the North, if the people shall place him in the executive chair of the nation," William Burgett to William Seward, 20 February 1860, Papers of William H. Seward, Reel 59.

[10] Invitations to a Seward dinner were issued usually a week before the event via a brief hand-written note sent in the mail. Responses were equally brief. For a dinner scheduled for February 10, 1860, an aide

to Winfield Scott wrote back "Liet. General Scott accepts with great pleasure Governor Seward's invitation for Tuesday next." No title, *New York Tribune*, 16 March 1860, p. 6; Winfield Scott to William Seward, 3 February 1860, Papers of William H. Seward, Reel 59.

[11]Glyndon G. Van Deusen, *William Henry Seward* (New York: Oxford University Press, 1967), 217.

[12]Three days before Seward delivered his address, Charles Anderson Dana, managing editor of the *New York Tribune,* informed him: "We shall, of course, publish it in all editions of the Tribune, but we wish to include it among our campaign tracts." "From Boston," *Springfield Daily Republican*, 3 March 1860, p. 1; Charles Anderson Dana to William Seward, 26 February 1860, Papers of William H. Seward, Reel 59.

[13]"From Washington," *New York Herald*, 10 May 1866, p. 6.

[14]Doris Kearns Goodwin, *Team of Rivals—The Political Genius of Abraham Lincoln* (New York: Simon & Schuster, 2005), 241.

[15]Ibid, 240-41.

[16]Ibid, 229.

[17]"Half Fare to the Convention," *Chicago Tribune*, 5 May 1860, p. 1.

[18]Goodwin, *Team of Rivals*, 239.

[19]"The Great Wigwam," *Chicago Tribune,* 14 May 1860, p. 1; "Our Chicago Correspondence," *New York Herald*, 15 May 1860, p. 3; "The Great Wigwam," *Chicago Tribune*, 3 May 1860, p. 1.

[20]The extended coverage of Lincoln's 1858 campaign and subsequent debate appearances was particularly effusive in the *Chicago Tribune,* which enjoyed a large circulation throughout the Midwest, but also in a number of New York newspapers where Seward was thought to be the most popular. See in particular, "Great Republican Demonstration," *Chicago Tribune,* 12 July 1858, p, 1; "Lincoln At Home," *Chicago Tribune,* 2 November 1858, p. 1; "The Contest in Illinois," *Rochester Daily Democrat*, 21 August 1858, p. 2; "Triumph

in Illinois," *Poughkeepsie Eagle,* 27 November 1858, p. 2; "The Canvass In Illinois," *New York Tribune,* 8 October 1858, p. 6; Roy P. Basler, *The Collected Works of Abraham Lincoln, Volume II* (New Brunswick: New Jersey, 1953), 461-69.

[21]"Abraham Lincoln," *Chicago Tribune*, 23 February 1860, p. 2.

[22]"The Presidential Campaign," *New York Herald*, 28 February 1860, p. 2.

[23]Roy P. Basler, *The Collected Works of Abraham Lincoln, Volume III* (New Brunswick: New Jersey, 1953), 522-50.

[24]No title, *New York Tribune,* 27 February 1860, p. 4.

[25]"Mr. Lincoln in New Hampshire," *Chicago Tribune*, 8 March 1860, p. 2; "The Campaign in New Hampshire," *New York Herald*, 5 March 1860, p. 10; "Lincoln in Connecticut," *Chicago Tribune*, 15 March 1860, p. 2.

[26]Isaac Pomeroy to Abraham Lincoln, 28 February 1860; Portland Republican Committee to Abraham Lincoln, 2 March 1860; both in Abraham Lincoln Papers, Reel 6.

[27]Basler, *The Collected Works of Abraham Lincoln, Volume IV,* 31.

[28]James Babcock to Abraham Lincoln, 8 April 1860, Abraham Lincoln Papers, Reel 6.

[29]Ira Buck to Abraham Lincoln, 6 April 1860, Abraham Lincoln Papers, Reel 6.

[30]Basler, *The Collected Works of Abraham Lincoln, Volume IV,* 49.

[31]"The Chicago Convention," *New York Tribune*, 14 May 1860, p. 5.

[32]William B. Hesseltine, *Three Against Lincoln—Murat Halstead Reports the Caucuses of 1860* (Baton Rouge: Louisiana University Press, 1960), 147.

[33]"National Republican Convention," *Indianapolis Journal,* 18 May 1860, p. 2.

[34]Hesseltine, *Three Against Lincoln,* 157; "Republican National Ticket," *Indianapolis Journal,* 19 May 1860, p. 2.

[35]Elbridge Spaulding to William Seward, 15 May 1860, Papers of William H. Seward, Reel 59.

[36]Elbridge Spaulding to William Seward, 16 May 1860, Papers of William H. Seward, Reel 59.

[37]Elbridge Spaulding to William Seward, 17 May 1860, Papers of William H. Seward, Reel 59.

[38]"The Chicago Convention," *New York Herald,* 18 May 1860, p. 1; "The Chicago Conv.," *New York Tribune,* 15 May 1860, p. 5.

[39]William Butler to Abraham Lincoln, 14 May 1860, and Mark Delahay to Abraham Lincoln, 14 May 1860; both Abraham Lincoln Papers, Reel 6.

[40]David Davis and Jesse Dubois to Abraham Lincoln, 15 May 1860; Unsigned to Abraham Lincoln, 18 May 1860; both Abraham Lincoln Papers, Reel 6.

[41]Mark Delahay to Abraham Lincoln, 17 May 1860, Abraham Lincoln Papers, Reel 6.

[42]Basler, *The Collected Works of Abraham Lincoln, Volume IV,* 50.

[43]"Republican National Ticket," *Indianapolis Journal,* 21 May 1860, p. 2.

[44]"The Chicago Convention," *New York Tribune,* 19 May 1860, p. 7.

[45]"The Chicago Convention," *New York Herald,* 19 May 1860, p. 3.

[46]Hesseltine, *Three Against Lincoln,* 171.

[47]"Republican National Ticket," *Indianapolis Journal,* 21 May 1860, p. 2.

[48]Gilbert Davidson to William Seward, 18 May 1860; Lewis Benedict to William Seward, 19 May 1860; both Papers of William H. Seward, Reel 59.

[49]Arthur Dexter to William Seward, 19 May 1860; Charles Sumner to William Seward, 20 May 1860; both Papers of William H. Seward, Reel 59.

[50]"The Republican Convention," *Springfield Daily Republican*, 23 May 1860, p. 2; Goodwin, *Team of Rivals*, 249.

[51]J. B. Pierce to Abraham Lincoln, 4 June 1860, Abraham Lincoln Papers, Reel 6.

[52]George Ashmun to Abraham Lincoln, 18 May 1860, Abraham Lincoln Papers, Reel 6.

[53]Lyman Trumbull to Abraham Lincoln, 18 May 1860; Schuyler Colfax to Abraham Lincoln, 18 May 1860; James Babcock to Abraham Lincoln, 19 May 1860; all Abraham Lincoln Papers, Reel 6.

[54]Thomas Hart Seymour to Franklin Pierce, 19 May 1860, Franklin Pierce Papers, Series 3, Reel 2.

CHAPTER FOUR

The Divided and Discordant Democrats

As George Ashmun and a group of boisterous Republicans happily boarded the Illinois Central heading due south to Springfield on May 19, an eastern Tennessee marshal was pondering the current depressing state of the Democratic party.[1]

"I am not one of those who have said I would not vote for Douglas if he were nominated," William Lowry explained in a letter to his pal Andrew Johnson. "I would go for him or any other good man."

But noting that most of his fellow Southerners hardly felt the same way, Lowry added: "I must think in the present disorganized state of things, Mr. Douglas could hardly do justice to himself to permit his name to stand before the country as a candidate, because if he is elected, it must be done by the South and it seems the South is very reluctant to take him up."[2]

One of the reasons why so many Southerners had come to detest Douglas was because Jefferson Davis told them to. At least that was the message they got as Davis eviscerated Douglas in yet another series of debates held in the Senate during the first two weeks of May, all of which were widely reported on in the Southern press.

In truth, the Davis-Douglas face-off did neither man much credit. Davis came off as a relentless stickler for detail with a prosecutor's zeal for winning. Douglas, on the other hand, simply seemed routinely maligned, endlessly trying to explain a dozen different controversial positions he had taken over a long career that in the end made him seem as though he was simply too compromised for the general election.

With the Senate galleries packed and warm, Davis unveiled his attack on May 7, ripping into Douglas for his role in the tumultuous Compromise of 1850 debates: "The Senator from Illinois and myself differed at that time, as I presume we do now," Davis proclaimed.

"We differed radically then. He opposed every position which I made," Davis added, as though this was in itself a sin, before pointing out that Douglas had voted against extending slavery into not only the territories but Mexico as well. Some of the Senate votes that Douglas cast back in 1850, Davis acknowledged, "He gave perforce of his instructions."

"But others of them," Davis made sure to add, "I think it is equally fair to suppose, were outside the limits of any instruction which could have been given before the fact."[3]

This could only mean one thing: Douglas and Douglas alone was responsible for the things that he said and the way that he voted. Therefore, he was unacceptable to the South.

Ironically, virtually all of the reasons that Davis used as reasons why Douglas would never prevail in the South were the same reasons why Douglas could be competitive in New York, Pennsylvania, Michigan, Indiana and his native Illinois.

But Davis wasn't speaking to the North. He rarely did. His target audience was his fellow Southerners, who had come to agree that Douglas was beyond hope.

For his part, Douglas, who when agitated looked like an obsessed pit bull and fought like one, too, attempted to defend himself, characterizing Davis' remarks as an "arraignment made of my political actions by the Senator from Mississippi." But even before he could really get going, Douglas was interrupted by Davis, who disdainfully retorted: "The reference to votes given by the Senator from Illinois does not seem to be exactly what might be termed a personal arraignment."[4]

Not until May 15 did Douglas finally have a full opportunity to mount his defense. Unfortunately, as he did, the country was distracted by the Republican convention in Chicago. Douglas nevertheless pushed on, delivering a speech that the *New York Tribune* thought was "marred by its prevailing egotism and personal application." It was also a speech that was nothing more than a reiteration of his long-held belief that the Constitution protected slavery as it existed and that the federal government should stay out of all slavery issues in the territories.[5]

For the next two days Douglas and Davis sparred. The nuances were sometimes maddening, but clearly showed that the smallest differences in national slave policy had become enough to distract the Democratic leadership, not to mention Democratic voters.

On May 17, Davis sought to get to the heart of matters when he bluntly asked Douglas if, as president, he would sign a bill to protect slavery in the territories.

Douglas: "It will be time enough for me, or any other man, to say what bills he will sign, when he is in a position to exercise the power."

Davis: "The Senator has a right to make me that answer. I was only leading on to a fair understanding of the Senator and myself about non-intervention."

Douglas: "I do not choose to begin to catechize the Senator from Mississippi."

Davis: "I shall not ask you a question further than you wish to answer; certainly not."

Douglas: "The Senator can ask all the questions he pleases, and I shall answer them when I please. But I was going to say that I do not recognize the right to catechize me in this way. The Senator has no right to do it, after sneering at my pretentions to the place which he assumes I desire to occupy."

Davis: "It was not that I thought the Senator was on the high road to that place."

In this ongoing theater, well received in the gallery, the two Senate legends presented a contrast in styles: Davis, every cool inch an aristocrat; Douglas, once and forever the frustrated underdog.

Near the end of their confrontation that same afternoon, both Davis and Douglas, perhaps realizing that they had only made Democratic unity more elusive, tried to minimize the effect of their remarks.

"I was not speaking for others," Davis, rather incredibly, claimed. "I am only a small man."

Douglas quickly agreed: "So am I. I am not speaking for others either."[6]

But both men knew that they in fact spoke for millions of others: Democrats across the land who were increasingly convinced that their party was doomed to a colossal defeat. Only naturally some party chieftains by late spring began a search for someone, anyone else, to top the November ticket.

"A movement is afloat to bring about the withdrawal of Douglas at Baltimore," the *New York Herald* disclosed on May 23, contending that Douglas was no longer capable of bridging the divisions so conspicuously given voice to by Davis. Other observers thought things had gone beyond the point of no return, that the party, with its intensely personal internal feuding, was now incapable of rallying around *any* nominee. "Each wing of the Dem. Party here evidently would prefer your election," Schuyler Colfax, whose ear in Washington was always flat on the ground, gleefully reported on May 26 to Lincoln.[7]

Whatever comfort Lincoln gathered from such messages, combined with his own reading of Democratic disunity, he continued to feel that he could take nothing for granted, particularly within his own party.

As Ashmun and his fellow celebrants noisily invaded Lincoln's wood frame house to officially notify him of his nomination, Lincoln was thinking about the powerful Republicans of New York. Were they angry enough about William Seward's convention defeat to sit out the general election?

An early indication came from Seward himself who sent a letter to the New York Central Republican Committee declaring: "I find in the resolutions of the convention a platform as satisfactory to me as if it had been framed with my own hands."

As for the presidential and vice-presidential nominees of the Republican party, Seward, without much enthusiasm, promised "sincere and earnest support."[8]

True, Seward did not mention Lincoln or Hannibal Hamlin by name, but at least he was tentatively on board. Instinctively, Lincoln waited for several weeks until Seward had recovered from the shock of his Chicago defeat before coaxing him into active campaigning for the Republican presidential ticket.

Thurlow Weed also needed time to heal. But by June 10 he was talking with Lincoln. And even the influential Charles Sumner of Massachusetts, another Seward man, was friendly, writing Lincoln from Washington: "Be assured, my dear Sir, of the joy with which I look forward to the opportunity of mingling with yr. Fellow-citizens in welcome to you here at the National Capitol next 4th March."[9]

Meanwhile, those who could not be overtly converted to Lincoln's cause were in the process of being neutralized.

With Lincoln's blessings, Joseph Medill of the *Chicago Tribune* paid a call on James Gordon Bennett, the wealthy, powerful and unpredictable owner of the *New York Herald*.

Because the *Herald* enjoyed a healthy circulation in both the North and South, Bennett's political influence in 1860 exceeded that of any other publisher in the country. In 1852, after Bennett made a big splash backing Franklin Pierce for the presidency, he abruptly turned into a relentless Pierce critic when he asked to be named ambassador to France and Pierce ignored him. How much Bennett contributed to Pierce's failure to win re-nomination from his own party in 1856 was unknown, but certainly his paper's daily lambasting of Pierce didn't help.

Buchanan, more cognizant of Bennett's emotional needs, courted the publisher, giving him advance copies of speeches and inside tidbits about important Washington doings. In return, Bennett gave to Buchanan mostly positive coverage from a paper that was mostly negative to all politicians.

Lincoln read the *Herald* every day and was only too aware of Bennett's power. But knowing that the publisher sympathized with the South on the issue of slavery, Lincoln thought the best he could get from Bennett was a lack of opposition rather than outright support.

"No hope of reward was held out by me," Medill reported to Lincoln after meeting with Bennett. But he noted that Bennett regarded Lincoln as a "man of good and honest intention." Medill then suggested that if he went easy on Lincoln in the campaign, Bennett might enjoy unprecedented access to a Lincoln White House.

The maneuver worked: the *New York Herald* in the weeks to come gave Lincoln extensive and even flattering front page coverage, while relegating negative comment to the paper's editorial page in a way that Bennett would have never done for Pierce.[10]

New York was full of pitfalls for Lincoln: Former Whig President Millard Fillmore, who had run as a third-party candidate in 1856, receiving a healthy 22 percent of the vote, was rumored to be interested in trying the same thing again in 1860. Although Lyman Trumbull told Lincoln that "Mr. Fillmore's course excites no interest here," both men were clearly worried that if Fillmore, who had become increasingly anti-slavery in recent years, did run, he would cut significantly into Lincoln's vote, particularly in the Empire State.[11]

And still the perils of Stephen Douglas continued to preoccupy the Lincoln team. Despite his unpopularity in the South, there was no denying that Douglas was well organized in the same Northern states that Lincoln would need to win the election. "There is a pause in Pennsylvania & New Jersey that will continue until after the Baltimore nominations," James Harvey, a journalist and supporter, told Lincoln on June 5, adding: "Douglas has a strong hold on his party in both."[12]

A Douglas nomination, it went without saying, could be good for the Republicans because the Democrats who followed Jefferson Davis would never accept him. But a Douglas loss would not be such a bad thing either: "If D. [Douglas] should *not* be nominated," Thurlow Weed wrote to Lincoln on June 10, "we should have many of his friends with us."[13]

By mid-June, many Democrats had come to the conclusion that despite his many flaws as a national candidate, Douglas could not be denied the party nomination. His acknowledged overwhelming delegate lead heading into the Baltimore convention was one thing, but so was the fact that despite all of their grumbling to the contrary, the Southerners had simply failed to rally around one of their own. "I do not see any satisfactory solution of the difficulty," Davis candidly told Franklin Pierce on June 13. "If Northern men insist upon Douglas, we must be beaten and with such alienation as leaves nothing to hope for in the future of nationality in our organization."[14]

President Buchanan, one day after the Covode Committee released the findings of its exhaustive investigation into his administration, findings that accused him of corruption but strangely did not call for his impeachment, was equally gloomy about the probability of a Douglas nomination. "The unity and strength of the Democratic party is annihilated and Lincoln elected," Buchanan flatly predicted to Robert Tyler on June 18.

"This is not the worst," Buchanan continued. "The Democratic party will be divided and sectionalized, and that too on the slavery issue. Everything looks bad, not only for the party, but for the country."[15]

Quietly, some Democrats believed there might still be a solution, however improbable, to their problems. For several weeks the name of John Breckinridge of Kentucky had been mentioned as a possible compromise candidate who could unite the party while also energetically taking the general election battle directly to Lincoln.

Only 39 years old, Breckinridge was widely perceived as a moderate on the slavery issue--his religious family regarded slavery as evil. He had served in the U.S. House and was just recently elected to a Senate seat that would not become vacant until 1861. But Breckinridge also won pro-slavery support because, earlier in the year, he had delivered an uncharacteristically strongly worded speech in Kentucky condemning, among other things, Hinton Helper's *Crisis of the South*, the theory of racial equality and the notion that the South could continue to live happily with the North under current conditions: "It is vain to cry peace, peace, when there is no peace," Breckinridge dramatically declared in words that could not help but win the applause and hearts of the Southern die-hards.[16]

Breckinridge was serving out his final frustrating months as Buchanan's vice-president, pushed to the sidelines by a secretive president who had little desire to share power with anyone. During the Charleston convention, Breckinridge had loyally supported fellow Kentuckian James Guthrie, even after it was clear that Guthrie's campaign was going nowhere.

Now Breckinridge backers wanted to know: was he still locked into his support for Guthrie, or would he permit his name to be entered into the balloting at Baltimore?

Breckinridge, not taking the matter very seriously, said if his backers insisted upon running him at Baltimore he would consent. But he was roundly pessimistic about his chances, and blamed Buchanan for the low state of his fortunes. "The President is not for me except as a last necessity," Breckinridge complained to James B. Clay, the son of Henry Clay and a childhood friend, "that is to say not until his help will not be worth a damn; meantime I suffer under the imputation of being his favorite."[17]

As the delegates to the Democratic convention gathered in Baltimore, the *New York Herald* disclosed that Southern leaders were already prepared to bolt in order to form their own party and nominate Caleb Cushing for president and Davis for vice-president. Cushing, who would preside over the Democratic convention, angrily denied any interest, explaining to Franklin Pierce: "If my nomination and election were matters which depended upon my pre-consent, that consent could not be obtained."[18]

Meanwhile those who opposed Douglas from within the party continued to hope that somehow he could be prevented from obtaining the two thirds delegate vote necessary for nomination, allowing someone else—Davis, Guthrie, Breckinridge, or even Andrew Johnson—to step in as a compromise candidate.

It was a prospect that Douglas thought possible, too, writing to one of his top campaign lieutenants, William Richardson, that he was open to the idea of "withdrawing my name," in favor of anyone who both promised to honor the Charleston platform and had a realistic chance of beating Lincoln. Douglas said essentially the same thing to Dean Richmond, another campaign leader, adding: "I beseech you in consultation with our friends to pursue that course which will serve the party and the country, without regard to my individual interests."[19]

Neither of the Douglas correspondents, devoted to him, would even consider the idea of withdrawing his name. Instead they hoped to simply put him over as quickly as possible, picking up last-minute delegates with the argument that the Douglas momentum was unstoppable.

As bands played on the streets in front of Barnum's Hotel, the Eutaw House, Mann's Hotel and the Gilmore House—almost anywhere the delegates were rooming—the mood in Baltimore seemed on the surface to be strongly, if mechanically, pro-Douglas. "The talk about the hotels was principally favorable to Mr. Douglas, whose friends were full of confidence and determination," noted Murat Halstead on the first day of the convention. A reporter for the *Charleston Mercury*, walking the same cobblestone streets busy with carriages of arriving delegates and loud talks made by the Douglas men, concluded: "All of the speeches were favorable for the nomination of Douglas."[20]

With its brick warehouses and old row houses, Baltimore in 1860 had a blue collar, ethnic-based population of more than 210,000 and was a familiar place for the Democrats, who had held six previous conventions in the city. This year,

Baltimore had also been the home to the creation of a new national political organization, the Constitutional Union Party, which was dedicated to easing sectional differences.

Meeting briefly during the second week of May inside the large First Presbyterian Church on Fayette street, the mostly elderly delegates to this third party convention debated beneath a huge portrait of George Washington and a series of large American flags.

But it soon became apparent that there wasn't much to debate. Party leaders purposely wanted to keep things as ambiguous as possible. They issued no platform and nominated for president former Tennessee Senator John Bell, who in his letter of acceptance would only say that he was for the "Maintenance of the Constitution and the Union against all imposing influences and tendencies."[21]

It was noted that Bell, whose stands and opinions over a long public career had been remarkably elastic, was 64 years old, more than a dozen years Lincoln's senior and that his running mate, the famous orator and former Massachusetts Senator Edward Everett, was 66, making the Constitutional Union party ticket the oldest in the field.

Democrats were not particularly worried about the Constitutional Union Party: "It enlists no particular interest here or in N.Y.," Jeptha Fowlkes, writing from Philadelphia, told Andrew Johnson. Much more threatening was the prospect of a Southern fourth party being organized, should Douglas be nominated.[22]

Meeting at the large Front Street Theater, Democratic delegates spent several rainy days arguing over credentials in an atmosphere thick with recrimination. Everyone was in a lousy mood, noted the *New York Herald,* which observed at least "five disgraceful fights, attended with more or less serious danger to the parties concerned." A reporter for the *Indianapolis Journal* watched one delegate from Arkansas threaten another delegate with a pistol. When a Pennsylvania delegate accused a Virginia delegate of hoarding tickets for the convention floor, he was hit with a "stinging blow in the face that brought the 'claret' in profusion."[23]

It took four days for the delegates to settle all of the credentials disputes. In the end, it was agreed that the vast majority—but not all—of the Southern delegates who had bolted at Charleston would be allowed to ballot at Baltimore. But the Louisiana and Alabama delegations, both of which had departed from Charleston as units, were not let back in.

This was all that it took for the Virginia delegation to take a walk. And they were soon followed by individual delegates from North Carolina, Tennessee, Kentucky and Missouri. Caleb Cushing, seeing where things were going, announced that he could no longer serve as convention president. "With what is left, Douglas will undoubtedly be nominated," the reporter for the *Indianapolis Journal* correctly perceived.[24]

On Saturday, June 23, the balloting was a foregone conclusion. Douglas won 181.5 out of the 191.5 delegates still voting. A move was made that Douglas' vote be declared unanimous. In what some delegates hoped might be a sign of late-blooming unity, Representative John Clark of Missouri, who had led the charge against John Sherman, Hinton Helper and the *Crisis of the South* in the winter, seconded the motion.

After eight years and two previous tries, Douglas was at last the presidential nominee of the Democratic party. But the party was in a shambles, with anger flowing in every direction.

On a train leaving Baltimore, Halstead sat next to a Douglas man from the North who said he could no longer tolerate Southerners: "After all the battles we have fought for the South, to be treated in this manner—it is ungrateful and mean." A large number of the Southern delegates were equally angry, charging that the Northern Democrats had forced Douglas upon them with little regard to their own feelings.[25]

Before Douglas even had a chance to formally accept his nomination, the dissident Southerners, meeting at the Maryland Institute Hall on East Baltimore Street, named Cushing as the president of their convention, and quickly nominated both Breckinridge as their standard bearer and Oregon Senator Joe Lane for vice-president on yet a fourth party ticket. Breckinridge couldn't believe the news and initially declared that he would not be a part of any campaign that would so thoroughly destroy the Democratic party. But a visit from both Davis and Cushing convinced him that his candidacy would in reality strengthen the Democrats by forcing Douglas out of the race and opening the way for the party to select a more competitive nominee.

"I trust I have the courage to lead a forlorn hope," Breckinridge finally agreed.[26]

The Breckinridge candidacy was naturally a thing to be savored by Republicans. Schuyler Colfax, describing the Democratic party as "divided & discordant," measured the impact of the Breckinridge campaign in Indiana, reporting to Lincoln: "No ticket could have been nominated of the seceeders better calculated to divide the Indiana Democracy [Democratic party] & open the state to you than Breckinridge & Lane."[27]

Douglas, in his acceptance speech on June 24, decided to address the question of the Southern revolt directly, arguing that a Southern exit from the national Democratic party only guaranteed Lincoln's victory, a result that would then lead to the secession of Southern states from the union.

"Can the seceders fail to perceive that their efforts to divide and defeat the Democratic party, if successful, must lead directly to the secession of the Southern states?" Douglas asked. "I trust that they will see what must be the result of such a policy and return to the organization and platform of the party before it is too late to save the country," he added.[28]

The swift, dramatic division in the Democratic party, with two presidential candidates running as Democrats—Douglas officially was the nominee of the Democratic National Party, while Breckinridge would head up the National Democratic party—created clear battle lines. At a huge and noisy rally in Washington, Buchanan noted that because Douglas and Breckinridge had both been nominated by partially-attended Democratic conventions, this made them equals.

"I have ever been the friend of regular nominations. I have never struck a political ticket in my life," Buchanan declared, before doing just that by striking at the Douglas ticket with his endorsement of Breckinridge and Lane.

"They have served their country in peace and in war," Buchanan declared, suddenly finding great merit in the vice-president he had ignored for nearly four years. "They are statesmen as well as soldiers, and in the day and hour of danger they will ever be at their posts."[29]

At an earlier Washington rally, Davis issued an uncharacteristically enthusiastic endorsement of the Breckinridge-Lane ticket, working up his audience with a summons: "Our cause is onward. Our car is the Constitution. Our fires are up. Let all who would ride into the haven of a peaceful country come on board. And those who will not, I warn that the cow-catcher is down—let stragglers beware."[30]

Franklin Pierce was also excited, releasing a public letter on June 29 in which he called into question the legitimacy of Douglas' nomination and revealed: "It would gratify me exceedingly if our friends in all sections of the land could unite earnestly and cordially in the support of Mr. Breckinridge and General Lane."[31]

Breckinridge was additionally endorsed by former president John Tyler, who remarked "If this be treason, make the most of it," and William Yancey, spiritual leader of the Democratic secession movement. Andrew Johnson, who had little use for secessions movements, instantly recognized the grass roots strength of Breckinridge in Tennessee and also lent his support.[32]

Perhaps the most humiliating Douglas defection came in the person of the reform-minded Alabama Senator Benjamin Fitzpatrick. Under pressure from Yancey partisans, Fitzpatrick took the extraordinary step of turning down the vice-presidential nomination on the Douglas ticket given to him by the regular Democrats in Baltimore.

Watching so much of the political base that could usually be taken for granted for any Democratic presidential nominee evaporate, Douglas was still not without assets. The powerful Tammany Hall, with the enthusiastic coordinated support of New York Mayor Fernando Wood and the young, emerging boss, William Tweed, came out for Douglas during a massive rally made deafening by sky rockets and Roman candles on July 2. And even though his long-time friend Theodore Miller told Martin Van Buren on July 5 that he doubted whether either "Douglas or Breckinridge in the present state of the case can carry a single Southern state," the former president also fell into line behind Douglas.[33]

Douglas additionally had the organized support of the regular party structure in any number of Northern states (although some state central committees were pumping for Breckinridge), prompting a *New York Herald* reporter to observe on July 16 that if those organizations could deliver for Douglas, "He will prove himself sufficiently powerful to break down the secessionists of the South."[34]

A surprising asset was additionally discovered in the man eventually selected by the Democratic National Executive committee as Douglas' new running mate: 48 year-old Herschel Johnson, the former popular governor of Georgia, who ignored the threats of the Yancey faction in his state and not only accepted the vice-presidential nomination, but promised an active campaign. Hung in effigy in Macon, Johnson was nevertheless determined to win converts to his cause. A correspondent for the *New York Herald,* polling voters in Georgia, would soon note that although Johnson's followers at the beginning of the campaign "could be scarcely numbered by tens," they would be "counted by the hundreds and thousands" by autumn.[35]

Meeting in New York during the first week of July with top Democrats, including the wealthy August Belmont, who promised to raise funds for his campaign, the sometimes-ecstatic, sometimes-depressed Douglas was ecstatic again, noting that William Richardson had just returned from a tour of the New England states.

"He reports things much better than we had hoped for," Douglas told newspaper editor Nathaniel Paschall. "He thinks we will certainly carry Maine, New Hampshire, Rhode Island

& Conn. Our friends in Penn & New Jersey are embarrassed by the action of the Central Committees of those states, but will form tickets on our own platform & fight boldly for victory."[36]

Uniquely, Douglas, facing challenges from all sides, now decided to do what no presidential nominee had done before: he would wage an active campaign in both the North and the South. It did not matter that Democrats in the North were increasingly attracted to Lincoln or that Democrats in the South regarded Davis as their spiritual mentor. Douglas was probably the only man in America who had faced off against both Abraham Lincoln and Jefferson Davis in person, and now he thought he could easily do battle with their followers and ideas across the country.

"The reaction in our favor is immense," Douglas remarked, contrary to all available evidence, "and we are gaining everyday."[37]

CHAPTER FOUR ENDNOTES

[1]"Mr. Lincoln at Home," *Chicago Tribune,* 22 May 1860, p. 2.

[2] William Lowry to Andrew Johnson, 19 May 1860, Andrew Johnson Papers, Reel 39, Series

[3]*Congressional Globe*, 1939-41.

[4]Ibid., 1970-71.

[5]"The Latest News," *New York Tribune*, 16 May 1860, p. 4.

[6]*Congressional Globe,* 2147, 2156.

[7]"Important from Washington," *New York Herald*, 2 June 1860, p. 2; Schuyler Colfax to Abraham Lincoln, 26 May 1860, Abraham Lincoln Papers, Reel 7.

[8]"A Visit to Springfield," *Chicago Tribune*, 31 May 1860, p. 2; "Noble Letter from Mr. Seward," *Springfield Daily Republican*, 23 May 1860, p. 2.

[9]Charles Sumner to Abraham Lincoln, 8 June 1860, Abraham Lincoln Papers,, Reel 7.

[10]Joseph Medill to Abraham Lincoln, 5 July 1860, Abraham Lincoln Papers, Reel 7.

[11]Lyman Trumbull to Abraham Lincoln, 8 June 1860, Abraham Lincoln Papers, Reel 7.

[12]James Harvey to Abraham Lincoln, 5 June 1860, Abraham Lincoln Papers, Reel 7.

[13]Thurlow Weed to Abraham Lincoln, 10 June 1860, Abraham Lincoln Papers, Reel 7.

[14]Jefferson Davis to Franklin Pierce, 13 June 1860, Franklin Pierce Papers, Series 3, Reel 6.

[15]Lyon G. Tyler, *The Letters and Times of the Tyler—Volume II* (New York: DaCapo Press, 1970), 55859.

[16]William C. Davis, *Breckinridge—Statesmen, Soldier and Symbol* (Baton Rouge: Louisiana State University Press, 1974), 207-08.

[17]Ibid, 221.

[18]"The Baltimore Convention," *New York Herald*, 17 June 1860, p. 5; Caleb Cushing to Franklin Pierce, 7 June 1860, Franklin Pierce Papers, Series 3, Reel 6.

[19]Robert W. Johannsen, *The Letters of Stephen A. Douglas* (Urbana: University of Illinois Press, 1961), 492-93.

[20]William B. Hesseltine, *Three Against Lincoln—Murat Halstead Reports the Caucuses of 1860* (Baton Rouge: Louisiana State University Press, 1960), 185; "The Baltimore Convention," *Charleston Mercury*, 20 June 1860, p. 4.

[21]"The Baltimore Convention," *Springfield Daily Republican*, 10 May 1860, p. 4; "National Constitutional Union Convention," *Charleston Mercury*, 14 May 1860, p. 4; "Mr. Bell's Letter of Acceptance," *New York Tribune*, 9 May 1860, p. 7.

[22]Jeptha Fowlkes to Andrew Johnson, 19 May 1860, Andrew Johnson Papers, Reel 39, Series 1.

[23]"The Disgraceful Scenes at Baltimore," *New York Herald*, 23 June 1860, p. 6; "Democratic National Convention," *Indianapolis Journal*, 25 June 1860, p. 2; "Democratic National Convention," *Indianapolis Journal*, 26 June 1860, p. 1.

[24]"The Baltimore Catastrophe," *New York Tribune*, 26 June 1860, p. 6; "Democratic National Convention," *Indianapolis Journal*, 29 June 1860, p. 2.

[25]Hesseltine, *Three Against Lincoln*, 263.

[26]"News from Washington," *New York Herald*, 30 June 1860, p. 7; Davis, *Breckinridge*, 224-27.

[27]Schuyler Colfax to Abraham Lincoln, 25 June 1860, Abraham Lincoln Papers, Reel 7.

[28]"Mr. Douglas' Speech after the Nomination," *Springfield Daily Republican*, 26 June 1860, p. 2.

[29]"President Buchanan's Speech," *New York Tribune*, 12 July 1860, p. 5; "Position of Mr. Buchanan," *New York Herald*, 26 June 1860, p. 6.

[30] Lynda Lasswell Crist, *The Papers of Jefferson Davis—Volume 6, 1856-1860* (Baton Rouge: Louisiana University Press, 1989), 357-60.

[31]"Ex-President Pierce on the Presidency," *New York Times,* 18 July 1860, p. 3; Franklin Pierce to B. F. Hallet, 29 June 1860, Franklin Pierce Papers, Series 3, Reel 6.

[32]"Notes of the Campaign," *Springfield Daily Republican*, 28 June 1860, p. 4.

[33]"The Tammany Ratification Meeting," *New York Herald*, 3 July 1860, p. 1; Theodore Miller to Martin Van Buren, 5 July 1860, Martin Van Buren Papers, Reel 34, Series 2.

[34]"The Presidential Problem," *New York Herald*, 17 July 1860, p. 1.

[35]"Gov. Johnson's Plantation," *New York Herald*, 26 September 1860, p. 2.

[36] Johanssen, *The Letters of Stephen A. Douglas,* 497.

[37] Ibid.

CHAPTER FIVE

―――――――

The Whole Surplus Energy of the Party

That the South had become a defensive place quick to action since John Brown's unsuccessful raid was seen on the afternoon of July 27 in the quiet northern Virginia village of Occoquan, where a banner bearing the names of Lincoln and Hamlin was instantly labeled as a "public offense and social affront" by outraged community leaders.

"Lincoln and Hamlin are but meaningless words in themselves," the *Alexandria Gazette* proclaimed. "But when displayed as they were at Occoquan, they represented principles at war with our tranquility and safety."[1]

It was bad enough that the banner promoted Lincoln, since his nomination by the Republicans generally regarded in the South as even a more dangerous radical than William Seward. But what made things worse was the addition of Hamlin, whose olive-colored skin was all it took to convince Robert Barnwell Rhett of the *Charleston Mercury* that he was not white.

"Hamlin is what we call a mulatto," Rhett declared during an early July Breckinridge rally, adding that he was outraged that the Republicans dared to "place over the South a man who has Negro blood in his veins."[2]

The Lincoln-Hamlin banner, raised by a small and brave group of local Republicans, quickly drove local and state officials to comic distraction. When it was additionally reported that a former slave had also taken part in the raising ceremony, it was clear that something would have to be done. General Eppa Hutton, in command of the Virginia guard, declared that he would risk his life to make certain that not only the banner but the pole it was raised on was removed.[3]

After a county court in nearby Brentsville declared the banner incendiary, a cavalry under the order of Governor John Letcher rode into Occoquan and surrounded the pole. To several anti-Lincoln villagers fell the task of axing the pole into pieces. The cavalry then took the banner into its possession, and presented it to the Brentsville court as evidence (although evidence of exactly what no one said).[4]

That one small banner in a remote village could create so much havoc said much about a region of the country that had become maniacally sensitive to the smallest differences of opinion, and was deadly determined to act first and ask questions later.

A case in point was the story of the young James Power. An Irish resident of Philadelphia, Power found work in Columbia, South Carolina as a stone cutter helping to work on the new statehouse there. One evening, while drinking with some of his fellow workers, Power casually disclosed that he had been sympathetic to abolitionism in the North and had become only more convinced of its cause since living in the South.

This was, for Power, a big mistake. Someone told someone else about his disclosure and before the young laborer knew what was happening, he was arrested and thrown in the Columbia city jail where for a week he was left to ponder his fate. At last, the marshal released Power. As he did so, he pushed him in the direction of several black men and yelled: "You god-damned son of a bitch. You are so fond of Negroes, I'll give you a Negro escort."[5]

Two black men then led Power three miles through the city on the way to a nearby railroad junction. As they did, Power noticed townspeople, including both city officials and state legislators, gathering along either side of the road, laughing and cheering.

At the junction, where the crowd now massed, Power was tied to a post and stripped. One of the black men was ordered to whip him, beginning an ordeal of 39 lashes, before an onlooker poured a bucket of hot tar on Power.

Some in the crowd called for Power's lynching, but he was instead pushed onto a freight train heading for Charleston, where once again local officials locked him up before sending him to New York by way of steamer

National newspaper readers in early 1860 no sooner got done absorbing the barbarity of the young Power's assault than reports of the fate of the elderly Daniel Worth were transmitted. A 65 year-old minister, Worth had boldly stated for years that he was against slavery in his native Virginia. But not until he was discovered handing out copies of Hinton Helper's *Crisis of the South* did Worth go from being a simple nuisance to an enemy of the state.

Noting that almost anyone in the South who held a contrary view on slavery was instantly labeled as an insurrectionist, Worth tried to explain that he never in fact talked with any slaves on the theory that there wasn't much that they could do about their condition. But he did talk regularly with some slaveholders, and not without results: "A slaveholder who has read this book is now asking his neighbors what he must do about his slaves," Worth reported to the anti-slave Boston Tract Society, adding "Are these not blessed portents?"

In fact, the portents, at least as far as Worth was concerned, were anything but. Arrested and tried in Asheboro, North Carolina, Worth was found guilty of "Speaking words calculated to make colored people uneasy." Trying to keep a good humor about him, Worth joked that because both he and Missouri Representative John Clark, for entirely different reasons, had done so much to keep the *Crisis of the South* in the news, they should get a cut of Helper's royalties.[6]

But few in the angry courtroom crowd were amused. Instead there were cries that Worth should be whipped and hung. The judge, taking note of Worth's age and perhaps reluctant in a religious part of the country to kill a man of the cloth, instead sentenced him to a year in jail.

Increasingly, Southerners looked twice at any unfamiliar visitor, particularly if that visitor had a Northern accent. "Let a strict watch be kept on all those freedom shriekers among us who are ever watching for an opportunity to run off slaves and are actuated by no other motive than a devilish desire to incite the Negroes to insurrection," warned the *Memphis Appeal*.[7]

At the same time slaveholders checked and re-checked the doings of their slaves (and even non-slave-holding whites were worried), convinced that John Brown insurrections were being plotted in every sun-baked work field by day and darkened cabin by night.

In Alexandria, Louisiana, a plantation master overhead his slaves cavorting late at night and wondered what all the excitement was about. Even though Sunday evenings traditionally were time off for many slaves, allowing them to hunt for food in the vicinity of their plantations, this seemed like a particularly rowdy gathering, made even noisier when slaves from another nearby plantation arrived.

The slaveholder decided on the spot that the two groups of slaves were obviously "Consulting together, planning mischief or insurrection." Offering only the most recent proof that the slaves' word-of-mouth system for transmitting news was just as effective as what was in the daily newspapers—which they were not allowed to read anyway—several of the slaves were also heard to be "Hurrahing for Lincoln.".[8]

The meeting was instantly broken up.

Just as troubling as latent slave enthusiasm for Lincoln was the Republican nominee's impact on slave prices. Traders maintained that if in the wake of a Lincoln victory all slaves would be freed, this must be factored into their asking price. "The depreciation amounts already to a hundred dollars a head on average," reported the *Charleston Mercury*, although rewards for a run-away slave remained high, with owners asking as much as $150 for a slave's capture and return.[9]

Feeling besieged from every corner, Southerners by early July turned to John Breckinridge as their only electoral salvation. "The news we receive from all portions of the state," reported *Nashville Union* editor John Burch to Andrew Johnson on Breckinridge support, is "in the highest degree encouraging."[10]

That perception was shared by many Democrats in the North: "If any candidate among the four now in nomination is in the ascendant," wrote New Hampshire Democrat Abner Greenleaf to Franklin Pierce, "it is the Kentuckian."[11]

But Breckinridge supporters also realized that their candidate, moderate in both temper and policy, would only say so much on the campaign trail. On a tour of his native Kentucky in July, Breckinridge had even gone so far as to deny that he was for secession.

"I am an American citizen," Breckinridge explained, "a Kentuckian who never did an act or cherished a thought that was not full of devotion to the Constitution."[12]

Clearly the South needed someone with more fire. Jefferson Davis was out because he too, was against secession. So was Andrew Johnson. Responding to a call that perhaps only he heard, William Yancey, the volatile Alabamian who had led the Southern walk-out at both the Charleston and Baltimore conventions and subsequently helped engineer the nomination of Breckinridge on the National Democratic Party ticket, decided it was his duty to speak up.

Yancey had long been known throughout the South for his uncompromising position on slavery and state's rights. When he was only a boy, his stepfather, a New York abolitionist, sold the Yancey family's slaves and relocated the family to the North. Yancey bitterly resented the upheaval in his young life and by the time he was in his early twenties, moved back South, embracing as he did a militant approach to sectional differences and floating the idea that someday the South would have to go its own way.

Yancey would eventually serve two terms in Congress, but he was far more effective as an outside agitator. In 1858 a letter he had written was made public in which he declared: "We shall fire the Southern heart—instruct the Southern mind—give courage to each other, and at the proper moment, by one organized concerted action, we can precipitate the Cotton States into a revolution."[13]

Beginning in July, Yancey launched a well-publicized tour of the border states as well as New York that was designed to frame the Southern point of view in ways that Breckinridge could not. A gifted speaker with a pleasing sense of humor, Yancey made a powerful impression wherever he went, suggesting repeatedly that the right of secession might very well have to be exercised in the South if events so warranted.

Before Yancey began his journey, which he said he was doing only to promote Breckinridge, he tried to explain away his notorious "fire the Southern heart" letter, arguing that he was simply for preparing an organized resistance to aggression. Incredibly, some Yancey supporters said the "aggression" might mean the secession movement itself. But those who knew Yancey intimately knew that in the context of 1860 his "organized resistance" theory meant a Southern response to a Lincoln election.[14]

In Washington, Yancey won applause when he noted that even though the Republicans had an effective organization known as the "Wide-Awakes,"--which was composed of young men in uniforms conducting massive parades throughout the North for Lincoln—any trampling of Southern rights in the wake of a Lincoln victory would guarantee one result.

"They will find some men in the Southern states, gentlemen, sufficiently wide awake to meet them on the battlefield," Yancey said as the Washingtonians laughed and cheered. "A brave and true people, gentlemen, will fear no wide-awakes."[15]

At the Cooper Union in New York, Yancey delivered one of his most sensational addresses, telling a rowdy audience that he believed in the right of secession and that if his native Alabama, after a Lincoln victory, decided to leave the union, he would go with it.

"The Constitution itself reserved certain rights to the states and the one right that rose above all was that when the government was oppressive, they should have the right to form new governments," Yancey declared, as the New Yorkers both cheered and booed in response. If a President Lincoln dared to "coerce a sovereign state," Yancey added, he would personally "fly to the standard of that state."[16]

It was hard to tell from the roar of the audience if Yancey had won over many listeners. But after his speech the *New York World* noted that while Yancey had a reputation as a fire-eater in the South, he "spoke like a sincere man and a gentleman— with boldness, it is true, but with urbanity and dignity."[17]

From the perspective of the Douglas camp, the growing national prominence of Yancey was a good thing. Although he still believed he could be competitive in the South, Douglas realized that his presidential fortunes ultimately rested on winning population-rich states in the North. If Yancey's appearance on the campaign trail might scare potential Northern Breckinridge supporters into supporting Douglas, so much the better.

During the second week of July Douglas began a sweeping tour of New England, trying to solidify support among Democrats in the one region of the country where he figured Breckinridge was the weakest. Speaking to a crowd of some 8,000 people outside the Revere Hotel in Boston on July 17, Douglas also cleverly framed his candidacy as the reasonable, moderate alternative between two political extremes.

"On the one hand you find a great Northern sectional party appealing to the North against the South," Douglas said to the mostly working class Irish gathering. "On the other hand you find a sectional party southward, appealing to the prejudices of the South against the North."

"The Republican party demand possession of the federal government in order that its power may be wielded for the prohibition of slavery where the people want it," Douglas continued. "The Southern sectional party demand possession of the federal government in order that the whole power of the government may be wielded for the defense and maintenance of slavery where people don't want it."[18]

This is how it would be for the duration of the Douglas campaign: smoking cigars, drinking whiskey, regaling reporters and speaking in public squares, town halls and even the back of a horse-driven wagon, Douglas would make his case. Repeatedly he asserted that his party, "occupying the safe, conservative middle ground," as he told a group of several hundred supporters in Springfield, Massachusetts on July 20, was the only party "demanding that the people themselves shall settle this question for themselves."[19]

At the statehouse grounds in Concord, New Hampshire on July 31, Douglas went on the attack against both Lincoln and Breckinridge for suggesting that the slavery issue could be ultimately decided one way or the other by the federal government. It was up to the people to "make their own laws and to establish institutions to defend themselves," Douglas asserted.

Arguing also that the slavery question should be decided by the people of Kansas for their own state and not by politicians in Washington, Douglas wondered why the newly-transported voters of Kansas appeared to suddenly lose their rights upon "crossing the Missouri River."[20]

In Rhode Island on August 3, Douglas attended a clambake at Rockey Point, arriving with a cigar in his mouth and cane in his hand. When asked to speak, he responded in a light vein, revealing, as he eyed the clams, why he was such a durable politician: "I haven't had a chance to try 'em yet. Among my youthful indiscretions I suffered myself to be elected judge, and one of the principles on what I used to act was in every case to demand the best evidence the nature of the case demands."

"Now, if there is one particular virtue in your clams over any other state, all I have to say is," Douglas then yelled: "*bring 'em on*."[21]

As Douglas moved his campaign southward, rumors were spreading of a possible combined or fusion ticket with Breckinridge. Northern Democrats, unwilling to cede New York, Pennsylvania and Ohio, increasingly wondered if the names of Douglas and Breckinridge could be printed on one ballot in order to forge a united front against Lincoln.

On July 19, the *Journal of Commerce* reported on a secret meeting of top Democrats at New York's Twelfth Avenue Hotel, the purpose of which was to set the groundwork for a fusion ticket that would then be ratified by the state's Democratic convention in August. The fact that officials with the Bell-Everett campaign also seemed interested in joining the effort gave hope to Democrats everywhere.

"The first and most important duty," the newspaper said of the varying factions, "they regard as the defeat of Mr. Lincoln and his party."[22]

The fusion movement also won the support of President Buchanan and Jefferson Davis, both of whom thought a series of combined tickets on the various state ballots was the only hope now of stopping Lincoln.

But even though Douglas was cordial to Bell, who he thought might take conservative votes away from Lincoln, he categorically refused to negotiate with Breckinridge, declaring "I have fought twenty-seven pitched battles since I entered public life and never yet traded with nominations or surrendered to treachery."[23]

Douglas' refusal to bargain enraged Davis, who later angrily described the candidate as a "grog-drinking, electioneering demagogue," while ruefully confiding to Franklin Pierce: "It must be that we have been doomed to destruction."[24]

Fusion's failure left the nation's former presidents struggling: John Tyler was downcast: "It seems certain to me that Lincoln is to be elected." Millard Fillmore, wary of both the Democrats and Republicans, came out quietly but not with much enthusiasm for Bell. Meanwhile, Martin Van Buren, still hoping for Douglas, could chuckle over at least one place where fusion seemed to be having an effect, receiving a letter from his old friend Francis Blair who reported on his own son's efforts thus far to retake his congressional seat in Missouri: "The partisans of every presidential candidate in the field in response, Bell, Breckinridge & Douglas, agreeing on nothing else, agreed to defeat him & he boldly denounced the whole & slavery to boot."[25]

For Republicans, the collapse of the fusion movement could only mean one thing: "You will be elected president," David Davis bluntly wrote to Lincoln on August 12 from Pennsylvania as he kept tabs on the Republican get-out-the-vote effort in that state. "There is no longer a doubt about it in my opinion."[26]

Thurlow Weed was equally optimistic, doubting that even a fusion ticket could stop Lincoln. Even if "*all* the factions were to united against us," Weed predicted, Lincoln was going to prevail in November. 27

But the good news about the collapse of the fusion movement was almost too good for Senator Henry Wilson, who reported to Lincoln on Republican enthusiasm in his home state of Massachusetts: "The people are disposed to listen and to go many miles to attend meetings," noted Wilson, who nevertheless added: "All this is very well, but I fear our friends are too confident and neglect organization. I fear our friends are trusting to the divisions of the Democracy, and to talk, and neglect work."[28]

Lincoln agreed, telling Wilson that the organization of various Lincoln campaigns at the state level involved "so much more of dry and irksome labor," that most volunteers "shrink from it—preferring parades, and shows, and monster meetings."

"I know not how this can be helped," Lincoln continued. "I do what I can in my position, for organization; but it does not amount to so much as it should."[29]

Organizing at the precinct and ward level would prove to be a challenge for both the Lincoln and Douglas campaigns throughout the fall. The Breckinridge and Bell organizations, with few volunteers on the ground, would rely nearly entirely on word-of-mouth and campaign event press coverage.

But the Lincoln men did try something different. On August 8 their man made a brief appearance at the Illinois State Fair in Springfield, arriving in a carriage that was, noted a reporter for the *Chicago Tribune*, quickly engulfed by "shouting and cheering supporters" who behaved "like mad men." Escorted through the mob, Lincoln spoke in only the most general terms to an audience of nearly 75,000 people, noting that "It has been my purpose since I have been placed in my present position to make no speeches."[30]

Instead, he relied upon the national press through a series of in-depth personality profiles to help spread his message, and that message was that Abraham Lincoln was a modest man of modest means who represented a rough pioneer democracy at its most romantic.

Such profiles inevitably made mention of Lincoln's unassuming wood frame home, the outside garden and neat fence, his gracious wife Mary and the candidate's relaxed bearing. That he looked so much like a working man with his tall, slender frame and massive hands, and seemed so amiable, with his endless jokes, not unlike a friendly neighbor down the street, all greatly favored an image that to many represented the classic American male and inevitably led to published stories that couldn't have been improved upon by the publicity office of the Republican National Committee.

"He rises far above the politician, he is a stranger to all of the intrigues which have cursed party politics," read one highly flattering profile in the *Philadelphia North American*, which was quickly re-published in the larger *New York Tribune*, adding "He is thoroughly imbued with the true elements of statesmanship and in the highest and noblest sense, he is a man."[31]

Neither Douglas, Breckinridge, nor Bell, received this kind of coverage; narratives that suggested that somehow Lincoln was just a better human being altogether and operated at a higher moral plan than the other three candidates combined because he was (contrary to all evidence) so apolitical.

But the Lincoln team, aware that both Douglas, and to a lesser extent Breckinridge, were daily in the news because they were willing to campaign, decided to also hit the hustings—only without Lincoln. Instead they recruited other Republican leaders to do the actual campaigning in Lincoln's place, serving two purposes at once by repeatedly getting Lincoln's message out before the voters without lowering him to the status of a mere candidate.

How such leaders would be used—and in some cases overused—was seen in a letter from Lincoln organizer Lyman Trumbull to Michigan Senator Zachariah Chandler, who was delegated to speak for Lincoln in Paris, Illinois as well as a variety of towns in Indiana.

"I do not know whether you would come to Chicago & there to Paris, or through to Indiana," Trumbull wrote. "I have written to N.B. Judd, the chairman of our State Central committee, that I presumed you would fill an appointment on the 16th on your way to Paris, if it can be so organized, that you reach Paris in time. I shall have a series of meetings arranged when we meet at Paris which will keep you plenty busy. Can you speak everyday? I suppose you could, if you do not care to do too much night traveling."[32]

All the Republican leaders campaigning for Lincoln, including Wilson of Massachusetts, Senator Benjamin Wade of Ohio, and German-American leader Carl Schurz of Wisconsin, would endure similarly punishing schedules.

But no one would drive themselves to the point of physical exhaustion as much as William Seward, who, beginning in early August, agreed to speak for Lincoln in a large number of states, and by so doing not only proved that he had moved beyond his painful defeat by Lincoln at the

Republican Convention, but was also smartly keeping his name in the news.

Arriving in Boston August 14, Seward showed that he was a good sport, alluding to his Chicago loss as an "unexpected surprise which has overtaken me," and adding, to great laughter: "It is God's will that we must be overruled and disappointed, and I have submitted with such graciousness as I can."

Seward then plunged into an energetic address in which he reminded his listeners not only of his famous "higher law" argument, but also of Massachusetts' long-standing opposition to slavery.

"What a commentary upon the wisdom of man is given in this single fact that fifteen years after the death of John Quincy Adams, the people of the United States who hurled him from power and from place, are calling to the head of the nation, to the very seat from which he was expelled, Abraham Lincoln," said Seward, "whose claim to that seat is that he confesses the obligation of that higher law which the Sage of Quincy proclaimed and that he avows himself."

In case anyone in the late night crowd was still uncertain as to Lincoln's abolitionist intentions, Seward declared to wild cheering: "I tell you fellow citizens that with this victory comes the end of the power of slavery in the United States."[33]

Seward expanded on this theme in Detroit on September 4 when he returned to the argument he had made the previous winter about slavery being a bad thing for both white and black people: "How natural has it been to assume that the motives of those who have protested against the extension of slavery was an unnatural sympathy with the Negro, instead of what it has always been—concern for the welfare of white people."

"There are few, indeed," Seward added to loud applause, "who ever realize that the whole human race suffers somewhat in afflictions and calamities which befall the humblest and most despised of its members."[34]

In Lansing two days later, after a lively Loud-Awakes torchlight parade, Seward remarked: "Slavery and freedom cannot exist in the same state, they are incompatible. There is an irrepressible conflict between them," before adding, without mentioning Lincoln, that a Republican victory was guaranteed only if "we take care not to suffer differences among ourselves or any other cause to divide us."[35]

Despite the obvious enthusiasm for Seward—at least 10,000 people turned out to hear him in Lansing—Republicans were still worried. When John Sherman campaigned for Lincoln in Philadelphia during the second week of September, he was roundly booed by local Democrats and John Bell supporters who rang cowbells, one of the symbols of the Bell campaign. One protestor yelled out "How about the Helper book?" Sherman, in response, altered somewhat his position from the one he had taken during the winter fight over the Speakership. He now said that he had indeed endorsed the *Crisis of the South*, and had "never regretted, and did not now regret" doing so.[36]

Republicans were also concerned about a rumored division within their ranks in Pennsylvania, a division that could conceivably give their state to Douglas, and a strong Democratic showing at the legislative level in, of all places, Illinois, which would be mortifying to the party. Contemplating the possibilities, Lincoln remained calm, telling one supporter that "No one thing will do us much good in *Illinois*, as the carrying of *Indiana* at the October election. The whole surplus energy of the party throughout the nation should be bent upon that object up to the close of the election."[37]

In fact, those early October elections not only in Indiana, but also pivotal Ohio and Pennsylvania, consumed Republican party officials who, as early as August, poured money and volunteers into the three states in the hope that a series of Republican state office victories would create an unstoppable momentum for the larger national elections in November.

But first came the Maine election, where Douglas hoped the Democrats might at least make a good showing. Lincoln, too, was concerned about Maine, telling Hannibal Hamlin that a loss of any of the state's congressional districts would "put us on the down hill track, lose us the state elections in Pennsylvania and Indiana, and probably ruin us on the main turn in November."

Showing his comfort in commanding, Lincoln closed his correspondence with an order to his running mate: "You must not allow it."[38]

The results of the Maine election showed that Lincoln was too pessimistic and Douglas not enough so: the Republicans swept the state, winning everything in sight.[39]

By the time of the Maine ballot, Douglas decided to launch his counteroffensive, with the goal of directly chipping away at Breckinridge's support in the South. Arriving by steamer to Norfolk on August 25, Douglas and his attractive wife Adele were escorted by an enthusiastic band of young black and white boys to the National Hotel. He would make national headlines the next day when, speaking from the front steps of a local court house, Douglas was asked whether or not the South would be justified in seceding if Lincoln won the election.

Bluntly—and perhaps without thinking of the political impact of his remarks in the South—Douglas answered: "To this I emphatically answer no."

He continued: "The election of a man to the presidency of the United States by the American people, in conformity with the constitution of the United States, would not justify any attempt at dissolving this glorious confederacy."

It may have been Douglas' greatest moment on the campaign trail, and he followed that up by reminding his audience that "I, as in duty bound by my oath of fidelity to the Constitution, would do all in my power to aid the government of the United States in maintaining the supremacy of laws against all attempts to break the union, come from what quarter it might."[40]

Probably no words could have done more to seal Douglas' fate in the South. He would, for example, be the first Democratic presidential nominee in history to lose Virginia. But his supporters in Norfolk and other places in the South said they admired his pluck, and as he subsequently spoke in Petersburg and Richmond (in the latter city he even dared to denounce Yancey), and finally Raleigh, North Carolina, it seemed like Douglas was making progress. A reporter for the *New York Herald* would even suggest that Douglas was "making a most favorable impression on the impassible—not irrepressible—minds of the Breckinridge men."[41]

Ending his Southern tour in Baltimore, where he would be greeted by more than 2,000 cheering supporters, Douglas could briefly believe that he might be turning things around. "Hon. Stephen A. Douglas was received in this city with a welcome which but few of the public men of this country have elicited," enthused the *Baltimore American* on September

7 in a prominent front-page story. "It was hearty, cordial and enthusiastic."[42]

But by the time of Douglas' Baltimore stop, Breckinridge had launched his own campaign during an outdoor rally in Lexington, admitting that "the circumstances under which I appear before you are novel and unusual," before delivering an address that attacked Douglas, charging that he was nominated by a Democratic convention where "whole states were excluded and disfranchised" for the single purpose of "forcing a particular dogma upon the Democratic organization."[43]

For the most part, Breckinridge's long speech was an excessive rebuttal of charges that had come to greatly anger him, suggesting that, like Yancey, he was a die-hard secessionist.

Repeatedly, Breckinridge denied those charges.

"Born within sight of this spot, known to you for near forty years, your representative in the legislature, in Congress, and having held other situations of trust," Breckinridge told his noon-day crowd of supporters, "I invite anyone to point to anything in my character or antecedents which would sanction such a charge or an imputation…I proudly challenge my bitterest enemy to point to an act, to disclose an utterance or to reveal a thought of mine hostile to the constitution of the United States."[44]

Breckinridge's speech was an odd one, as was his campaign strategy, which came more into focus after he travelled around Kentucky. While he defiantly insisted that he was not a secessionist, Breckinridge's support came most prominently from those who supported secession. Focusing entirely on Douglas and rarely mentioning Lincoln, he seemed much more intent on securing his position with the Democratic party and nation as he appealed to a section of the country more than willing to abandon both.

Despite the mixed message of Breckinridge's campaign, his following among Southerners was undeniable. Even before Breckinridge's strange opening salvo, Southerners still loyal to Douglas admitted, with no small degree of despair, that Breckinridge had become the most popular choice in their region. Hershel Johnson, Douglas' running mate, looked over the Southern political landscape and candidly envisioned defeat: "I have not much hope for the future. The sky is dark." Former Georgia Congressman Alexander Stephens, also one of the few remaining voices for Douglas in the South, told a group of supporters: "The signs of the times portend evil and everything seems to be tending to national disruption and general anarchy."[45]

Recognizing, as the Lincoln men did, the importance of the coming state elections in Pennsylvania, Ohio and Indiana, Douglas moved his entourage to Harrisburg on September 7, where he again condemned Breckinridge as a party-wrecker and ripped into home-stater President Buchanan for abandoning tariff policies that he said had protected the workers of Pennsylvania.

From there, Douglas went to Reading, where he once again said he would not join in a fusion ticket with Breckinridge. "I can never fuse and never will fuse with a man who tells me the Democratic creed is dogma, contrary to reason and the constitution."[46]

On September 12, he took a quick detour through western New York, appearing at an ox roast in Jones Woods (Douglas at the very least was eating well), and again letting his sentiments be known about a possible Lincoln presidency. "I should regret the election of Abraham Lincoln as a national calamity. I know him well—very well. I have had good reason to know him, and he has still better reason to know me," said Douglas to laughs.

But if Lincoln ended up as the winner, Douglas vowed, the new president would be "bound by his oath to carry out the laws to their faithful execution…and I, as his firmest and most strenuous and most irreconcilable opponent, will sustain him."[47]

The Douglas party pushed into Elmira on September 14 and four days later was in Rochester, beginning a fast-moving journey through Ohio that would see the candidate address tens of thousands of enthusiastic admirers along the way. In Dayton, as he was beginning to lose his voice from giving up to a dozen speeches a day, Douglas again jabbed at both Lincoln and Breckinridge, saying he was thankful that he had no opinions that "cannot be proclaimed in the same terms everywhere, wherever the American flag waves over American soil."[48]

With the usually dour Herschel Johnson along for the ride, Douglas pulled into Indianapolis on September 29 where another crowd estimated in the thousands cheered him. There could be no doubt about it: the reception in both Ohio and Indiana had been good. Even Johnson allowed himself a brief moment of optimism, wondering if somehow Douglas, whose endurance seemed boundless, might still against all odds win.[49]

Certainly, thought Johnson, Democratic October wins in both of those states would dramatically alter the fundaments of the race.

The Republicans thought so, too, although Seward professed to be not worried, abandoning the Pennsylvania-Ohio-Indiana battle ground on September 14 to give speeches in Wisconsin, Minnesota, Iowa, Missouri and Kansas. He concluded this last tour on October 1, where he was greeted by Lincoln.[50]

Enthusiastically, Seward told the nominee: "We are happy to report to you, although we have traveled over a large part of the country, we have found no doubtful states."[51]

Seward was right—at least as far as Pennsylvania, Ohio and Indiana were concerned. They all produced Republican victories for state candidates on October 10. Those results were instantly seen as a precursor of what would most likely happen in the presidential election in November.[52]

"If we could sufficiently swell our voices they should ring over the land until Pennsylvania, Indiana and Ohio should hear us exulting over their noble victories," Trumbull remarked to an excited crowd that gathered outside Lincoln's home that night. "And if we can boast of these achievements in the vanguard of the fight, what shall become of the Democrats on the 6th of November, when our chief commander leads the battle?"[53]

Although the successful Republican gubernatorial candidates won only 53 percent in Ohio and 51 percent in Indiana, the Democrats now felt that the so-called "down-hill track" that Lincoln had worried about would be their fate for the duration of the campaign.

Douglas, recognizing that the results in those three states revealed real Republican enthusiasm, also acknowledged that with the probable loss of those states in November, he was doomed—although he continued to hold out hope for Illinois, where his friendships were legend.

Refusing to boast publicly, Lincoln in a quick note to Seward on October 12 remarked: "It now really looks as if the Government is about to fall into our hands. Pennsylvania, Ohio and Indiana have surpassed all expectations, even the most extravagant."[54]

CHAPTER FIVE ENDNOTES

[1]"The Occoquan Affair," *Baltimore American*, 31 July 1860, p.1

[2]"A Remarkable Discovery," *Baltimore American,* 19 July 1860, p.1

[3]"The Trouble at Occoquan, Virginia," *New York Herald,* 29 July 1860,

[4]"The Abolition Tree in Occoquan," *Richmond Dispatch,* 30 July 1860, p.1; "The Virginia Row-Do-Row," *Chicago Tribune,* 30 July 1860, p.1; "The Trouble at Occoquan, Virginia," *Springfield Daily Republican,* 30 July 1860, p.4.

[5]"An Irishman Scourged and Tarred and Feathered," *New York Tribune,* 2 January 1860, p.6; "An Irishman Tarred and Feathered," *Springfield Daily Republican,* 2 January 1860, p.2..

[6]"North Carolina Anti-Slavery Movement," *New York Tribune*, 12 April 1860, p.6; "The Case of the Rev. Daniel Worth," *New York Tribune*, 8 May 1860, p.1; "Reverend Daniel Worth," *National Anti-Slavery Standard,* 9 June 1860, p.1.

[7]"Abolitionists About," *Charleston Mercury*, 27 August 1860, p.4.

[8]"Abolition Fruits in Louisiana," *Charleston Mercury,* 13 August 1860, p.1.

[9]"Depreciation of Slave Value," *Baltimore American*, 30 October 1860, p.1; "One Hundred and Fifty Dollars Reward," *Charleston Mercury*, 9 July 1860, p.2.

[10]As Breckinridge's fortunes in Tennessee improved, Douglas' worsened: "Taking all Middle Tennessee together, there will not be, unless things are altered, one thousand votes for Douglas," Democratic insider Washington Whitthorne reported to Andrew Johnson on July 24. Leroy P. Graf, *The Papers of Andrew Johnson— Volume 3, 1858-1860* (Knoxville: University of Tennessee Press, 1972), 645-46; Washington Whitthorne to Andrew Johnson, 24 July 1860, Andrew Johnson Papers, Series 1, Reel 1.

[11]Abner Greenleaf to Franklin Pierce, 6 August 1860, Franklin Pierce Papers, Series 3, Reel 6.

[12]William C. Davis, *Breckinridge—Statesman, Soldier, Symbol* (Baton Rouge: Louisiana State University Press, 1974), 234.

[13]"Another Letter from Mr. Yancey," *Richmond Dispatch*, 1 August 1860, p.1.

[14]Ibid.

[15]"Speech of Hon. William L. Yancey," *Richmond Dispatch*, 24 September 1860, p.1.

[16]"Hon. Wm. L. Yancey in New York," *Baltimore American*, 12 October 1860, p.1.

[17]Ibid.

[18]"Douglas in Boston." *Springfield Daily Republican*, 19 July 1860, p.2; "From Boston," *Springfield Daily Republican*, 20 July 1860, p.2.

[19]"Mr. Douglas in Springfield," *Springfield Daily Republican*, 21 September 1860, p.2.

[20]"Movements of Mr. Douglas," *New York Herald*, 1 August 1860, p.5.

[21]"Senator Douglas at Rhode Island Clam Bake," *New York Herald*, 5 August 1860, p.8; "Douglas at a Clam Bake," *Richmond Dispatch*, 7 August 1860, p.1.

[22]"Important to Douglas Men," *Chicago Tribune*, 28 July 1860, p.2.

[23]Robert W. Johannsen, *Stephen A. Douglas* (New York: Oxford University Press, 1973), 793.

[24]Jefferson Davis to Franklin Pierce, 23 November 1860, Franklin Pierce Papers, Series 3, Reel 2.

[25]Francis Blair was running as a Republican to recapture his seat in Missouri's 1st Congressional district, which included St. Louis, and would win in the general election with 44 percent against two other candidates. Lyon G. Tyler, *The Letters and Times of the*

Tylers—Volume II (New York: Da Capo Press, 1970), 561-63; Frank Severance, *Millard Fillmore Papers, Volume Two* (Buffalo: Buffalo Historical Society, 1907), 379-80; "The Hon. Millard Fillmore," *Columbus Daily Enquirer*, 28 August 1860, p.2; Francis Blair, Sr. to Martin Van Buren, 10 August 1860, Martin Van Buren Papers, Reel 34, Series 2.

[26]David Davis to Abraham Lincoln, 12 August 1860, Abraham Lincoln Papers, Reel 8.

[27]Thurlow Weed to Abraham Lincoln, 13 August 1860, Abraham Lincoln Papers, Reel 8.

[28]Henry Wilson to Abraham Lincoln, 25 August 1860, Abraham Lincoln Papers, Reel 8.

[29]Roy P. Basler, *The Collected Works of Abraham Lincoln, Volume IV* (New Brunswick: Rutgers University Press, 1953), 109.

[30]"Lincoln at Home," Chicago *Tribune*, 9 August 1860, p.1.

[31]"Interesting Political News," *New York Herald*, 12 August 1860, p.8; "An Evening with Abraham Lincoln," *Springfield Daily Republican*, 14 July 1860, p.2; "A Visit to Lincoln," *New York Tribune*, 23 August 1860, p.7; "Hon. Abraham Lincoln at Home," *New York Herald*, 13 August 1860, p.5.

[32]Lyman Trumbull to Zachariah Chandler, 3 October 1860, Papers of Zachariah Chandler, Reel 30.

[33]"Senator Seward Down East," *New York Herald*, 15 August 1860, p.1.

[34]"Political Issues of the Day," *New York Tribune*, 5 September 1860, p.5.

[35]Not everyone who heard Seward speak was impressed. J. Mannon, a member of the Wide-Awakes in Michigan, reported to Zachariah Chandler after listening to Seward's address: "I told Gov. Seward that I would not flatter him—that he did not speak as well as Senator [Benjamin] Wade. (But his speech reads well)."; "The Great Political

Crisis," *New York Herald*, 8 September 1860, p.10; J.Mannon to Zachariah Chandler, 6 September 1860, Papers of Zachariah Chandler, Reel 1.

[36]"The Hon. John Sherman in Philadelphia," *New York Times*, 15 September 1860, p.1.

[37]Basler, *The Collected Works of Abraham Lincoln, Volume IV*, 116-17.

[38]In response, Hamlin maintained that the state's 3rd and 6th congressional districts, which the Republicans won respectively in 1858 by 50.2 percent and 51.5 percent, might prove close. Basler, *The Collected Works of Abraham Lincoln, Volume IV;* Hannibal Hamlin to Abraham Lincoln, 8 September 1860, Abraham Lincoln Papers, Reel 8.

[39]"The Maine Election," *New York Times*, 11 September 1860, p.1. In the 3rd and 6th districts that most worried Hamlin, the Republicans marginally improved their 1858 vote, winning with 52.5 percent and 53.9 percent.

[40]"Movements of Senator Douglas," *Baltimore American*, 28 August 1860, p.1; "Douglas on the Stump," *Charleston Mercury*, 3 September 1860, p.4.

[41]"Douglas in North Carolina," *Baltimore American,* 5 September 1860, p.1; "Judge Douglas in Virginia," *New York Herald*, p.1.

[42]"Mr. Douglas in Baltimore," *Baltimore American,* 7 September 1860, p.1.

[43]"Meeting at Lexington," *Louisville Daily Courier*, 6 September 1860, p.1.

[44]Ibid.

[45]Johannsen, *Stephen A. Douglas*, 784; "Hon. A.H. Stephens on the Stump for Mr. Douglas," *Baltimore American,* 3 September 1860, p.1.

[46]"Movements of Mr. Douglas," *New York Tribune*, 8 September 1860, p.7; "The Presidential Canvass," *New York Herald*, 9 September 1860, p.1.

[47]"The Presidential Campaign." *New York Times*, 13 September 1860, p.1.

[48]"The Pilgrim's Progress," *New York Times*, 29 September 1860, p.4.

[49]"Douglas Here," *Indianapolis Journal*, 28 September 1860, p.2.

[50]"Senator Seward's Western Tour," *New York Herald*, 19 September 1860, p.2; "The Great Contest," *New York Herald*, 26 September 1860, p.2; "Mr. Seward on the Missouri Border," *Springfield Daily Republican*, 2 October 1860, p.2.

[51]Lincoln was initially invited to greet Seward at a Chicago reception scheduled for October, but decided instead to receive him in Springfield. ""Senator Seward's Tour in the West," *New York Herald*, 1 October 1860, p.5; Alexander Harvey to Abraham Lincoln, 14 September 1860, Abraham Lincoln Papers, Reel 8.

[52]"Election News," *Indianapolis Journal*, 11 October 1860, p.2; "State Elections," *Columbus Gazette*, 12 October 1860, p.3.

[53]"Pennsylvania and Indiana," *Chicago Tribune*, 13 October 1860, p.1.

[54]Lincoln was responding to an October 8 letter from Seward in which he reported on the favorable political prospects for a Republican win in New York, remarking "I find no reason to doubt this State will redeem all the promises we have made." Basler, *The Collected Works of Abraham Lincoln, Volume IV*, 126-27; William Seward to Abraham Lincoln, 8 October 1860, Abraham Lincoln Papers, Reel 8.

CHAPTER SIX

Madness Rules the Hour

Running out of options, Stephen Douglas decided to suspend his campaign in Pennsylvania, a state that was draining his resources with, as seen by the October elections, little tangible result.

The move was welcomed by the Breckinridge men who thought that with Douglas out of the picture their man might be able to beat Lincoln there. That notion prompted long-time Democratic insider John Forney to scoff: "That Pennsylvania will vote for Abraham Lincoln on the first Tuesday in November is as certain as fate."[1]

As Douglas once again brought his campaign to the South, Franklin Pierce tried one last time to salvage the fortunes of the anti-Lincoln forces, writing to Pennsylvania Democrat James Campbell: "The true dangers to the Union to result from Mr.

Lincoln's election are greater than any of us are willing to anticipate, and yet I have not seen, and do not know how the calamity is to be averted."

Pierce had an idea, which may have seemed far-fetched given how late it was in the campaign. Both Douglas and Breckinridge, eating into one another's support, should simultaneously withdraw, he said. Then the regular Democrats could come together in yet a third convention and nominate Kentuckian James Guthrie for president along with Horatio Seymour, former governor of New York, as vice-president.

Kentucky and New York—the party would again be united.

"It is not too late to retrieve our fortunes and defeat sectionalism," Pierce added.[2]

But Douglas remained uninterested in all such machinations. He arrived in Memphis on October 23, leading a squadron of horses down streets thick with onlookers who were noticeably subdued.

The lackluster response, so different from the cheers Douglas received in Virginia in August, provided evidence that if his campaign really was collapsing in the North, there was little reason for remaining Douglas enthusiasts in the South to risk the wrath of their neighbors by supporting him.[3]

The flat Southern response to Douglas seemed even more noticeable when compared to the excitement now generated by the candidacy of Breckinridge. A reporter in Louisville for the *New York Tribune* thought the Breckinridge campaign was resonating not only with the landed gentry but among regular working people as well, noting that Breckinridge had an "unbounded popularity with all classes in all of the states of the South."[4]

Some observers even thought that Breckinridge, sweeping the South, might actually beat Lincoln nationally if he could also win in New York and, as previously noted, Pennsylvania. Writing to David Gardiner, his brother-in-law in New York, John Tyler on October 27 crossed his fingers for Breckinridge, commenting: "I will not permit myself to abandon the hope that the large cloud which hovers over us will be dispersed through the action of your large and powerful state."[5]

At the same time, some overly enthusiastic Republicans in the South even began to believe that Lincoln might be more popular in the region than previously imagined. "From a knowledge of your general character as a statesman, I am satisfied that you are a real patriot & conservative," W. T. Early of Virginia wrote to Lincoln, also on October 27. Early added that Southern enmity regarding the Republican nominee was not personal and was most likely due to suspicions that he was just another William Seward.[6]

A more realistic appraisal of Southern opinions on Lincoln came from Alexander Stephens, watching with dread as the 1860 campaign neared its rancorous end. Stephens knew that Southerners hated Lincoln. He also knew that Breckinridge was on the verge of sweeping the South. Asked by a reporter how Southerners would respond should Lincoln win the election, Stephens was characteristically candid: Undoubtedly, he said, the South would leave the Union.[7]

Herschel Johnson, Douglas's running mate, thought the same thing, declaring: "In the South, particularly in the cotton states, there is a large body of intelligent, chivalrous, elevated, patriotic, true-hearted men that believe the election of the Republican candidate will be a sufficient cause for dissolution of the Union."

Mississippi Governor Albert Brown promised to call a special legislative session in Jackson with the purpose of entertaining a move to secede, while former Virginia Governor Henry Wise, unsure of what his state would do, said he was keeping an eye on developments in both of the Carolinas as well as Georgia, noting, "Any one state, even the smallest, can make the battle and win the victory."[8]

On October 31 a correspondent for the *New York Herald* in Richmond reported that matters were moving beyond simple talk: "Preparations in Virginia for the coming crisis are actively going on," he wrote, adding that "arms and ammunition are being rapidly distributed."[9]

Republicans, keeping an eye on the same developments, continued to downplay secession threats. In St. Louis, also on October 31, Francis Blair, Jr., writing for a group of local Republicans, told Lincoln "We are not among those who believe that the glorious Union will be sundered in consequence of the triumph of our party in the contest so close at hand." But Blair added that it was inevitable that at the very least "an attempt to dismember the Union" would be made.[10]

Soft-peddling secession threats, Republicans nevertheless began to worry about the effect such talk might be having on Wall Street. Speaking in front of the Merchants Exchange in New York, prominent banker James Gallatin tried to calm investor nerves by insisting that the election of Lincoln would be good for the economy. He asserted that businessmen in the South agreed, but were too afraid to say so publicly. Even so, William Cullen Bryant, influential editor of the *New York Evening Post,* suggested to Lincoln on November 1 that he issue a statement for Wall Street consumption which would, "as they say, 'quiet the public's mind.'"[11]

Lincoln rejected Bryant's advice. But his campaign dispatched Seward to the Palace Gardens in New York for a final, massive weekend rally. Taking his cue from Bryant, who sat at the dais behind him, Seward calmed investor jitters when he downplayed the secession threat: "I do not think these threats, before election, are evidence of revolution and disunion after election." he declared. A man who intends to strike a fatal blow, Seward added, does not usually "give notice so long beforehand."[12]

As Douglas wrapped up his campaign in Alabama, events underscored his lousy luck. Speaking at a mid-day rally from the steps of the state capitol in Montgomery, he was pelted with eggs. Undaunted, he plunged into his speech, declaring "I believe there is a conspiracy on foot to break up this Union. It is the duty of every good citizen to frustrate the scheme."[13]

Sitting in the audience as Douglas spoke was the inevitable William Yancey, just returned from his headline-making tour of the North and now promising to rebut in an evening address everything Douglas had just said. Douglas, on a tight schedule, could not stay to listen. Boarding a boat that would take him to Selma by way of the Alabama River, he and his wife Adele were injured when the deck they were standing on collapsed.

Speaking the next day in both Selma and Mobile, and once again drinking, Douglas was greatly annoyed when a Breckinridge supporter asked him if it was true that if Lincoln won he would serve in his cabinet. "There is no language with which I can express my scorn and contempt for this wretch who would intimate that in any contingency I would take office under Lincoln," he replied angrily.[14]

Douglas decided to stay in Mobile for election night, where he would read telegraph returns at the office of the

Mobile Register with a small group of supporters and the paper's editor, John Forsyth, Jr. Breckinridge retired to his Lexington residence to wait out the results, while John Bell, at his home off the Cumberland River near Nashville, quietly wondered if his ill-funded Constitution Union campaign might net him one of two border states.

In Springfield it was hard to get around as thousands of locals and visitors congregated on the streets of the town on election day, convinced that they were about to see history in the making. Bands playing military and patriotic songs from the back of horse-driven wagons also made the day noisy. Despite the outside chaos, Lincoln seemed removed from what was going on, holing up in the governor's room of the State House, which offered him a window view of a courthouse across the street where the balloting was taking place.

By late afternoon, Lincoln noticed that the crowds on the street were temporarily thinning and decided that it was a good time to cast his ballot. He made his way to the courthouse unnoticed, but as he entered the building someone yelled out his name and a number of people came to his side, one joking: "You ought to vote for Douglas, he has done all he could for you."[15]

A reporter for the *New York Tribune*, getting his first glimpse of Lincoln in person, took note: "His slenderness strikes one as even beyond what had been expected," he wrote, before observing that as Lincoln made his way back to the State House he "took off his hat and smiled all around."[16]

Lincoln ate dinner with his wife Mary and their two boys before returning to the State House early in the evening, waiting with a large group of supporters and fellow politicians for the latest telegraphic returns. Those dispatches would provide an exciting, panoramic view of the country, moving east to west, as the polls closed and the results were tabulated.

From New York, Thurlow Weed sent several messages addressed personally to Lincoln, one assuring him that his majority in the Empire State, despite the fact that he was losing the big Irish vote in New York City, was "nearly or quite 30,000." By morning Lincoln's margin of victory over Douglas in New York would actually exceed 50,000.[17]

From Pennsylvania, Simon Cameron wired: "Penn. Seventy-thousand for you. New York Safe. Glory enough." Again, Lincoln's numbers looked better by light of day, beating his nearest opponent Breckinridge by more than 90,000. Douglas' non-campaign there netted him 3.5 percent—his worst showing in the North.[18]

From Indiana, where Lincoln would win 51 percent to Douglas' 42 percent and Breckinridge's 4.5 percent, state Republican chairman John Defrees wired: "Large Republican gains. All safe."[19]

But not until Illinois reported later in the evening did Lincoln allow himself to feel hopeful, although he continued to worry about New York. Throughout the night he had cheered in response to victories of local Illinois Republicans in their respective races, growing quiet only when his own numbers came in. By late evening it was finally clear that Lincoln had won his home state, although only with 50.7 percent. Douglas scored his strongest showing in a Northern state with 47.2 percent—with the remaining 2 percent divided by Breckinridge and Bell.

The Constitution Union nominee, long regarded by the press as the most unimportant candidate in the presidential race, ended up having a surprisingly good night, winning almost 13 percent of the vote nationally, along with three border states, Virginia, Tennessee and Kentucky (the latter to the surprise of Breckinridge).

At the same time, projections of a Southern sweep for Breckinridge were on the mark. His national total was just over 18 percent and he won 10 states. Of those, eight were in the South where his vote ranged from a low of 44.9 percent in Louisiana to a triumphant high of 75.5 percent in Texas. In between, he carried Herschel Johnson's Georgia with 48.9 percent (his strongest opponent here was Bell with 40.3 percent) and Alabama with a solid 54 percent.[20]

The Republican performance in Congressional races was uneven: their numbers in the Senate jumped from 26 to 31; but in House elections, voters provided a classic presidential election corrective to the previous mid-term vote, decreasing the Republicans' totals from 114 to 105. Totals for the Democrats would not be known for weeks and were muddled by the fact that even though they were competitive in a tough election environment, the vast majority of their Southern members would resign their seats before the next Congress met, giving the Republicans complete control in both Houses by default.

Leaving the *Mobile Register* late in the evening, a downcast Douglas contemplated his depleted fortunes. He had won 29.5 percent of the national vote—the worst showing for a presidential nominee in the history of the Democratic party. His summer tour of New England won him nothing, where he was shut out by Lincoln and got his best vote in Rhode Island with 38.6 percent. His frantic and highly-publicized early October effort in Ohio and Indiana showed that voters in both states were at least receptive to his arguments, as he won an almost identical 42.3 percent and 42.4 percent respectively.

The South gave Douglas his worst totals, despite his summer and fall visits to the region. His vote ranged from 2.8 percent in North Carolina to 15.1 percent in both Louisiana and Alabama.

In the end, Douglas carried only two states nationally, New Jersey and Missouri, for a total of 12 electoral votes. Bell's three-state win was good for 39 electoral votes, while Breckinridge amassed, for a third party candidate, an impressive 72 electoral votes. 20

Lincoln knew, shortly after midnight when his New York victory was confirmed, that he was the president-elect. With Mary he attended a late night victory dinner sponsored by a group of Republican women where the men of Springfield ate everything in sight and the women, noted the *New York Tribune* reporter, "took possession of and clung to Mr. Lincoln when he appeared among them."[21]

Looking over reports sprawled before him the next morning, Lincoln could see that his caution on election evening had been well-placed. His total national vote was only 39.9 percent—the smallest popular vote for a presidential winner in nearly four decades. Douglas and Breckinridge combined won 47.6 percent—painful evidence to Franklin Pierce, Jefferson Davis and other traditional Democrats that Lincoln might very well have been defeated had the Democrats come together.

Like Lincoln, many partisans in the South could not be sure of the final result of the election until late on the evening of November 6 or even early the next morning. In Charleston, local townspeople jammed the small offices of the *Charleston Mercury* waiting for the news from New York. Once it was obvious that Lincoln had finally won the Empire State an immense crowd that had gathered outside the newspaper's office broke into cheers.[22]

As Robert Barnwell Rhett, Jr., would note the next morning, Lincoln's win, now making secession inevitable, was seen as liberation for the South. "The tea has been thrown overboard," said the *Mercury*, edited by Rhett. "The revolution of 1860 has been initiated."[23]

In fact, supporters of secession, primarily in South Carolina, had been waiting for this moment for months, if not years. On the day before the election, the South Carolina legislature met to receive a message from Governor William Gist who recommended the immediate drawing up of a special convention to consider secession.

In the weeks leading up to the election, Gist had even been in touch with his fellow Southern governors, trying to gauge secessionist sentiment in each state. The responses were promising: Alabama, Mississippi and Louisiana were willing to leave the Union, but each hoped to be a part of a coordinated regional response. Florida would go if South Carolina went first. Georgia was divided, although secession leaders felt they had the upper hand.

Now the South Carolina legislature voted overwhelmingly for a special convention to meet on December 17 to weigh secession, with one lawmaker, Representative Samuel McGowan, urging his fellow legislators to act promptly. "We have delayed for the last ten years," he said. "We thought it the best and wisest policy to remain in the Union with our Southern sisters in order to arrange the time when and the manner of going out."

With secession more tangible than ever before, McGowan contended that it would be "the height of madness" for South

Carolina to wait. The time to act, he said to thunderous applause, was now.[23]

As the South Carolina legislature made its historic move, firemen in Charleston armed themselves and began infantry drills. A foundry in the southern part of the state went to work on a local order of some 10,000 bullets. A letter was received in Charleston from Knoxville offering the services of "volunteer companies from Tennessee." Throughout the state the talk was suddenly no longer of simply seceding, but of a coming war.[24]

In Virginia, John Tyler was without hope. "I fear we have fallen on evil times, and that the day of doom for the great model Republic is at hand," he wrote on November 10 to his old friend, Silas Reed. "Madness rules the hour, and statesmanship in all its grand and massive proportions, gives place to a miserable demagogism which leads to inevitable destruction."

Already being touted for a leadership role in the secession movement, the only living ex-president from the South added: "I leave to others younger than myself the settlement of existing disputes."[25]

Jefferson Davis, relaxing at his Brierfield plantation, expressed to Rhett his doubts that Mississippi would, on its own, secede. But understanding Southern pride, Davis added: "If the secession of So. Ca should be followed by an attempt to coerce her back into the Union, that act of usurpation, folly and wickedness would enlist every true Southern man for her defence."[26]

By the time both Mississippi Governor John Pettis and Alabama Governor Andrew Moore expressed their open support for secession, Stephen Douglas was in New Orleans, recuperating from the campaign with his wife Adele and enjoying the food, music and drink of a city that seemed tailor-made for his pleasure.

Members of the city's conservative business elite, represented by the *Daily Picayune*, which suggested that the Southern states should "come calmly together" to exercise their rights under the constitution, were alarmed by the actions of the South Carolinians and invited Douglas to express his views on secession.[27]

Douglas promptly replied in a long public letter, declaring that "No man in America regrets the election of Mr. Lincoln more than I do; none made more strenuous exertions to defeat him." But as he said throughout the last days of the campaign, Douglas once again repeated: "The election of Mr. Lincoln, in my humble opinion, presents no just cause, no reasonable excuse for disunion."[28]

Douglas promised to have more to say on the topic when he returned in early December to Washington.

By the third week of November hotels in the nation's capital were reporting a brisk business as both pro and anti-secession enthusiasts arrived from all over the country to lobby their representatives. Reporters had a difficult time discerning a trend, some noting that Southern members of Congress, who had previously downplayed secession, now seemed inclined to support it. But a writer for the *New York Herald*, talking with lobbyists representing a variety of business and industry interests, discerned "decisive opinions against the legality of secession." Either way, the mood in the city was pensive, thought a *Chicago Tribune* correspondent, who observed: "People, at least such as you meet in the streets, look dejected, as though they had parted with their last copper and knew not where the next was to come from."[29]

In the middle of it all stood James Buchanan, already resentful over the numerous stories in the press suggesting that his presidency had been a colossal failure.

On the day after the election, the president was not at all certain that South Carolinian threats to secede were anything he should be very worried about. He had heard talk of secession many times before, he told friends, and had come to regard it as nothing more than rhetoric; empty words framed to keep Southern voters back home happy while simultaneously winning concessions from politicians of the North in Washington.

But now matters seemed more serious, primarily because so many old friends had taken it upon themselves to speak bluntly to the president.

"I deeply regret the embarassments which will surround you during the remainder of your term," Senator John Slidell of Louisiana wrote to Buchanan on November 13. "I need scarcely to say that I will do everything in my power to modify them."

But the idea that secession could now be prevented, continued Slidell, was folly: "I see no possibility of preserving the Union, nor indeed do I consider it desireable."[30]

Meeting with his cabinet on November 9, Buchanan had confronted divisions on the secession question even within his own administration.

Secretary of State Lewis Cass of Michigan wanted Buchanan to take a firm line as quickly as possible against the secessionists, worrying about re-enforcing federal forts along the coast of South Carolina should they be threatened. Secretary of War John B. Floyd of Virginia was against any action regarding the forts, and was causing more headaches for the president due to the many stories in the press regarding financial irregularities in War Department accounts. Secretary of the Treasury Howell Cobb of Georgia counseled patience, but found his own loyalty to the federal government wavering as a result of Lincoln's victory. Attorney General Jeremiah Black of Pennsylvania thought Buchanan had the right to protect the forts, but could not use force to keep South Carolina within the Union; while Interior Secretary Jacob Thompson of Mississippi argued the Southern line, but stopped short, for the time being, of endorsing secession.

Add into the mix vice-president Breckinridge, who would preside over the opening of the last session of the 36th Congress and was still suspicious of Buchanan, and the country was left with an administration defined by more than the normal divisions and intrigue.

Buchanan was blunt: he hoped only to hold things together long enough for Lincoln to take over. He desired nothing more than retreating to his pleasant Wheatland estate in Lancaster, Pennsylvania where he could do what he liked best, host lengthy dinner parties with guests capable of witty conversation, enjoy the best wines and latest books.

Such an obvious lack of interest in his job was seen by some as the primary cause of the secession crisis: "If that old thing at the head of affairs was worth anything," remarked Mississippian John Gettys in a letter to Thaddeus Stevens on November 15, "there would be no danger."[31]

Polling cabinet members and asking them what should be done about South Carolina, Buchanan only naturally received a wide variety of views, leaving him more troubled than ever. Scheduled to deliver his final and most important annual message to Congress on December 3, Buchanan slowly moved in the direction of condemning secession, but letting it happen; threatening military action if any federal property in the South should be seized, but maybe letting that happen too.

All of Washington wondered what he would finally say and Buchanan hardly made things any more clear when he met with a reporter for the *New York Herald* on November 22 and noted "South Carolina wishes to enter into a conflict with me—a conflict with myself—and upon the drawing of the first blood to drag other Southern states into the secession movement." He declined to reveal whether or not he had any plans for a military response, but then oddly added that if the Southerners should appeal to the North for fairness and the North failed to respond appropriately, he would cast his lot with the South.[32]

Whether or not Buchanan was telegraphing, in this interview, his support of the secession movement, many in the South still felt he had not said enough. On November 24 Rhett wrote the president to warn: "South Carolina, I have not a doubt, will go out of the Union—and it is in your power to make this event peaceful or bloody. If you send any more troops into Charleston Bay, it will be bloody."[33]

Two days later in a letter to Jacob Thompson that would be published in papers across the country, Franklin Pierce came out adamantly against any anti-Southern response from the White House, adding that the secession crisis anyway had been nearly entirely caused by a confrontational North. "Now, for the first time, men are compelled to open their eyes, as if aroused from some strange delusion, upon a full view of the nearness and magnitude of impending calamities," Pierce wrote.[34]

Given the divisions within his own cabinet and party, it seemed unlikely that Buchanan's annual message would be a bold document. Even so, what he finally sent to Congress proved to be a masterpiece of presidential inertia, declaring that if the country really was falling apart it was due entirely to the "long continued and intemperate interference of the Northern people with the question of slavery in the Southern states," an interference, the president said, which had finally "produced its natural effects."

In fact, continued Buchanan, for more than 25 years Northern aggression had created an environment of insecurity in the South, pushing it in the direction of secession: "Self-preservation is the first law of nature," Buchanan observed, before suggesting that the only real solution to the crisis was for the people of the North to stop harassing the people of the South.

He then addressed the central question being asked by everyone: would the federal government resort to military action should matters in the South get out of hand? Buchanan's response astonished the North: "Our Union rests upon public opinion and can never be cemented by the blood of its citizens shed in a civil war. If it cannot live in the affections of its people, it must one day perish. Congress possesses many means of preserving it by conciliation, but the sword was not placed in their hands to preserve it by force."[35]

Buchanan's only concrete proposal was for Congress to pass a constitutional amendment upholding the right to own a slave not only in the South, but also, incredibly, in the territories.

Buchanan's message left him open to the most severe criticism of his presidency. The *New York Tribune* said that the "indecision and hesitation" expressed in the document "show that he is unequal to the exigency and will evade any real responsibility."[36]

The *New York Times* was apoplectic. "It seems incredible that any man holding such a high official position should put forth such an argument," the paper began, charging that the message would "tend still further to exasperate the sectional differences of the day."

"The sum and substance of this message," said the *Philadelphia Press*, "amounts to a recommendation to the Southern states who believe themselves to be aggrieved, to leave the Union, and an encouragement that, in the event of their doing so, there is no authority to be found either in the Constitution or laws under it, to punish them or call them back."[37]

But William Seward got off the best take, observing that Buchanan's policy could now be boiled down to two uncompromising principles: "That no state has the right to secede unless it wishes to," and "That it is the president's duty to enforce the laws, unless somebody opposes him."[38]

Despite the president's obvious favoritism towards the South, Treasury Secretary Cobb thought Buchanan was still not pro-Southern enough and resigned five days after the message. Washington insiders saw it coming—Cobb was well-known as a secession enthusiast, so much so that immediately after quitting his job he boarded a train for Charleston to offer his help to the cause.

The resignation on December 12 of Cass as Secretary of State was a more serious matter. Although Buchanan publicly lauded Cass, in private he disliked the Michigander, regarding him, in a way that the president's critics might have found ironic, as too old and out of touch for his job. For his part, Cass could not believe that Buchanan might actually not protect the federal forts, and decided he could no longer be a part of the administration.

Just a little less than three weeks later, Secretary of War John B. Floyd would be the third member of Buchanan's cabinet to announce his resignation, after being indicted by a District of Columbia grand jury for mishandling War Department money.

Outsiders watching the disturbing implosion of the Buchanan presidency only naturally concluded that solutions to the secession crisis were most likely not going to be found in Washington. Several hundred New Yorkers who gathered at a federal courthouse in Buffalo on December 12 turned to former president Millard Fillmore for answers, asking him to serve as a special "commissioner of peace" to travel to the South and urge secessionists to stay in the Union.

Fillmore, in response, was candid: "This is certainly an honorable and patriotic mission and did I believe it could do any good, I should not hesitate a moment to undertake it."

But until Northern Republicans were willing to "treat our Southern brethren as friends," added Fillmore, such a trip would be useless.[39]

As the New Yorkers returned to their homes, feeling less hopeful than before, John Crittenden was in an optimistic mood. At 77 years of age, Crittenden had been a figure in national politics for more than half a century, representing his native Kentucky in both the House and Senate. He understood how to bring seemingly implacable parties together in the service of a greater cause: in 1850 as Attorney General he had helped then-President Fillmore broker the famous Compromise of 1850, the historic legislation recognizing Southern slavery, admitting California as a free state, and organizing the Utah and New Mexico Territories without restrictions on slavery.

Now Crittenden would head up a Senate committee designed to do the impossible: hammer out a new series of compromises designed to stave off secession and somehow return harmony to the country. Breckinridge, presiding over the Senate, picked the committee's members and could hardly be faulted for a lack of imagination. Robert M.T. Hunter of Virginia, earlier a candidate for the 1860 Democratic presidential nomination, and Lazarus Powell of Kentucky, would represent border state opinion that remained skeptical about secession. Jacob Collamer of Vermont, Benjamin Wade of Ohio, James Grimes of Iowa and James Doolittle of Wisconsin represented the Northern abolitionist point of view, although Doolittle was less interested in freeing slaves than in sending them to Africa.

The Northern Democratic view would be represented by William Bigler of Pennsylvania and Henry Rice of Minnesota, wary of both abolitionism and secession; while Robert Tombs of Georgia was there for a Deep South, pro-slavery, pro-secession perspective.

Then came the names that captured the imagination of the country: William Seward, Stephen Douglas and Jefferson Davis.

Seward, just then mulling over an offer by Lincoln to become his Secretary of State, was at first uninterested in what came to be called the Committee of Thirteen (a larger Committee of Thirty, devoted to the same mission, was formed in the House). But acknowledging that the body might actually stave off the crisis, Seward agreed to serve. Douglas, although still tired from the presidential campaign, signed on without hesitation.

That left Davis, who was the least inclined to join. He could see where the South was heading, his closest friends told him secession was now inevitable and slowly he had edged towards the idea himself, writing an open letter to his constituents on December 14 declaring that the Union was busted. Finally he relented. "If, in the opinion of others, it be possible for me to do anything for the public good," he remarked, he would serve "at the command of the Senate."[40]

On the same day that the Committee of Thirteen was created, Andrew Johnson rose in the Senate to present his take on matters. Since Lincoln's election, the Tennessee senator had been hearing from his constituents, many of whom viewed the secession movement as a top-heavy one, driven by aristocratic slaveholders like Jefferson Davis.[41]

Johnson, instinctively suspicious, had his own ideas. For days reporters had been guessing about Johnson's coming speech, pointing out rightly that it was almost impossible to predict which side in the sectional crisis he would ultimately take. That build-up now resulted in a packed Senate gallery which listened closely as Johnson proposed a series of Constitutional amendments requiring a sectional balance in the makeup of the Supreme Court as well as in all future presidential tickets. He additionally thought an agreed-upon boundary dividing slave from non-slave state (including all future states) all the way to the Pacific would go a long way in easing tensions.

But then Johnson let loose: "I am opposed to secession," he remarked as his fellow Southern senators listened in shock. "If the doctrine of secession is to be carried out upon the mere whim of a state, this government is at an end, it is not stronger than a rope of sand; its own weight will tumble it to pieces."

He then offered a lucid offensive against secession, noting "If a state can secede at will and pleasure," would not a majority of the states "under the compact they have made with each other," possess a similar right to "combine and reject any one of the states from the confederacy?"

Swiftly rejecting the impassioned and often loudly-stated assertions of his Southern colleagues, Johnson concluded that the states "have no such rights; the compact is reciprocal."[42]

Southerners were outraged by Johnson's speech. He was verbally assaulted on the streets of Washington. An Alabama resident named Hiram Smith wrote to warn Johnson that he would soon receive his "just deserts," adding: "No man with a drop of Southern blood in his veins would openly proclaim such doctrines."[43]

Johnson's old friend Blackston McDannel reported from Tennessee on a group of local Democrats who had been "trying for several days to get up a meeting to pass condemnatory resolutions in regard to your course and to burn you in effigy."[44]

Planning to return South in January, Johnson knew that his life was in danger. Secessionist fever had swept Tennessee, although much more so in the western than eastern half of the state. The excitement was only made the greater by the news coming out of Charleston on December 20: South Carolina had officially seceded.

Acknowledging this latest, historic development, the *Charleston Mercury* now began to list in their paper all newswire reports coming out of Washington under the heading of "Foreign News."[45]

The beginning of disunion was at hand.

CHAPTER SIX ENDNOTES

[1]"Pennsylvania Politics," *New York Times*, 20 October 1860, p. 1; "The Straight Douglas Men of Pennsylvania," *Chicago Tribune*, 20 October 1860, p. 1.

[2]Franklin Pierce to James Campbell, 17 October 1860, Franklin Pierce Papers, Reel 2, Series 1.

[3]"Douglas in Tennessee," *Charleston Mercury*, 20 October 1860, p. 4.

[4]"Effect of the October Elections in the South," *New York Tribune*, 19 October 1860, p. 7.

[5]Even if Lincoln should win, Tyler was not certain that that would automatically lead to secession, advising William Waller, a young Virginia cadet ready to resign his commission and offer his services to the South, to wait until "Virginia had distinctly and plainly mapped out her course after the election. If Mr. Lincoln is elected, and appearances all point strongly that way, disunion may not respectively follow. That is a question to be decided by the people of the States and many things may transpire to prevent disunion." Leon G. Tyler, *The Letters and Times of the Tyler, Volume II* (New York: Da Capo Press, 1970), 563; John Tyler to William Waller, 5 November 1860, John Tyler Papers, Reel 2, Series 1.

[6]W. T. Early to Abraham Lincoln, 29 October 1860, Abraham Lincoln Papers, Reel 10.

[7]"The Coming Struggle," *New York Herald*, 29 October 1860, p. 1.

[8]"Political," *Baltimore American*, 29 October 1860, p. 1.

[9]"The Revolution at the South," *New York Herald*, 3 November 1860, p. 5.

[10]Francis P. Blair, Jr. to Abraham Lincoln, 31 October 1860, Abraham Lincoln Papers, Reel 10.

[11]"Black Republicanism in Wall Street," *New York Herald*, 6 November 1860, p. 5; William Cullen Bryant to Abraham Lincoln, 1 November 1860, Abraham Lincoln Papers, Reel 10.

[12]"Grand Mass Meeting," *New York Tribune*, 3 November 1860, p.8; "Mr. Seward's Reply to the Threat of Disunion," *Springfield Daily Republican*, 5 November 1860, p. 2.

[13]"The Indignity to Douglas at Montgomery, Alabama," *Chicago Tribune*, 12 November 1860, p. 2; Robert W. Johannsen, *Stephen A. Douglas* (New York: Oxford University Press, 1973), 801.

[14]Johannsen, *Stephen A. Douglas*, 802.

[15]"Lincoln Votes for President," *Daily Picayune*, 11 November 1860, p. 4.

[16]"From the Home of Mr. Lincoln," *New York Tribune*, 10 November 1860, p. 6.

[17]Thurlow Weed to Abraham Lincoln, 7 November 1860, Abraham Lincoln Papers, Reel 10.

[18]Simon Cameron to Abraham Lincoln, 6 November 1860, Abraham Lincoln Papers, Reel 10.

[19]John Defrees to Abraham Lincoln, 6 November 1860, Abraham Lincoln Papers, Reel 10.

[20]All statistics taken from *Congressional Quarterly's Guide to U.S. Elections* (Washington: Congressional Quarterly, Inc., 1994), 377, 435.

[21]"From the Home of Mr. Lincoln," *New York Tribune* 12 November 1860, p. 5; "Mr. Lincoln Receives the News Quietly," *Springfield Daily Republican*, 9 November 1860, p. 2.

[22]"The News of Lincoln's Election," *Charleston Mercury*, 8 November 1860, p. 1.

[23]"The Crisis in the South," *Baltimore American*, 12 November 1860, p. 1; "Disunion Movements and Talk," *Springfield Daily Republican*, 15 November 1860, p. 2.

[24]"From South Carolina," *Richmond Dispatch,* 10 November 1860, p. 1; "Affairs at the South," *Richmond Dispatch,* 12 November 1860, p. 1.

[25]John Tyler to Silas Reed, 10 November 1860, John Tyler Papers, Reel 2, Series 1.

[26]Linda Lasswell Crist, *The Papers of Jefferson Davis, Volume 6, 1856-1860* (Baton Rouge: Louisiana State University Press, 1989), 368-71.

[27]"South Carolina—The Future," *Daily Picayune,* 13 November 1860, p. 5.

[28]"Mr. Douglas After His Defeat," *New York Tribune,* 15 November 1860, p. 5; Robert W. Johannsen, *The Letters of Stephen A. Douglas,* (Urbana: University of Illinois Press, 1961), 499-503.

[29]"Letter from Washington," *Daily Picayune,* 18 November 1860, p. 9; "The Reports from Washington," *New York Herald,* 14 November 1860, p. 1; "A Gallery Picture of Washington," *Chicago Tribune,* 15 November 1860, p. 1.

[30]Philip Shriver Klein, *President James Buchanan—A Biography* (University Park: Pennsylvania State University, 1962), 352.

[31]John Gettys to Thaddeus Stevens, 15 November 1860, Thaddeus Stevens Papers, Series 1.

[32]"Important from the South," *New York Herald,* 23 November 1860, p. 1.

[33]John Bassett Moore, *The Works of James Buchanan, Volume XI, 1860-1868* (New York: Antiquarian Press, 1960), 5.

[34]"Ex-President Pierce on the Political Crisis," *New York Times,* 3 December 1860, p, 1; Franklin Pierce to Jacob Thompson, 26 November 1860, Franklin Pierce Papers, Reel 2, Series 2.

[35]Moore, *The Works of James Buchanan, Volume XI, 1860-1868,* 7-43.

[36]"The President's Message," *New York Tribune,* 5 December 1860, p. 6.

[37]"The President's Message," *Baltimore American*, 6 December 1860, p. 1.

[38]Thaddeus Stevens was less whimsical than Seward, writing to his fellow Pennsylvania Republican Edward McPherson on December 19, he said simply: "Buchanan is a very traitor." "News and Gossip from Washington," *Springfield Daily Republican*, 8 December 1860, p. 4; Thaddeus Stevens to Edward McPherson, 19 December 1860, Thaddeus Stevens Papers, Series 1, Roll 1.

[39]"Millard Fillmore as a Commissioner of Peace," *New York Tribune*, 30 December 1860, p. 4; "President Fillmore to Gen. Dix," *New York Times*, 24 January 1861, p. 2.

[40]*The American Annual Cyclopedia—1861* (New York: D. Appleton & Company, 1862), 175.

[41]Representative of the eastern Tennessee ambivalence towards secession was a letter Johnson received from Samuel Williams of Trenton, Tennessee charging that secessionists "appeal to the passions and attempt [to] excite the popular mind relating grievances in their most aggrivated [sic] form." Samuel Williams to Andrew Johnson, 5 December 1860, Andrew Johnson Papers, Series 1, Reel 1.

[42]"From Washington," *Richmond Dispatch,* 27 December 1860, p. 1; *Congressional Globe, 36th Congress, 2nd Session* (Washington: John C. Rives, 1860), 117-20, 134-43.

[43]Hiram Smith to Andrew Johnson, 29 December 1860, Andrew Johnson Papers, Series 1, Reel 1.

[44] Blackston McDannel to Andrew Johnson, 29 December 1860, Andrew Johnson Papers, Series 1, Reel 1.

[45]"Foreign News," *Charleston Mercury*, 29 December 1860, p. 4.

CHAPTER SEVEN

———

Old Abe Has Landed Safely

On the morning of December 22, Speaker of the House William Pennington sent an important message by courier to Michigan Senator Zachariah Chandler, asking: "Will you do me the honor to dine today promptly at 6 p.m. & meet our friend Gen'l Scott?"[1]

Lieutenant General Winfield Scott had arrived in Washington during the second week of December, and was greatly alarmed. From his Army headquarters in New York, Scott had warned Buchanan about the precarious nature of federal forts along the South Carolina coast, among other locations in the South, noting "In my opinion, all these works should be immediately so garrisoned as to make any attempt to take any of them by surprise *coup de main* ridiculous."[2]

Overweight and probably suffering from both hypertension as well as diabetes, Scott, at 74, was also worried about possible plans to attack and seize control of Washington and what might happen to Lincoln during his outdoor swearing-in ceremony on March 4. In the days to come he would meet with Pennington, Chandler and Seward, all of whom shared his alarm, and President Buchanan, who didn't.

Scott later disclosed that he had received "more than fifty letters, many from points distant from each other," specifically containing threats to Lincoln.[3]

He was not the only one who was concerned. "That there is an infamous conspiracy on foot to take this city, the navy yard and especially the capitol, sometime in February, is no longer doubtful," a reporter in Washington for the *Springfield Daily Republican* wrote. Massachusetts attorney Abram Randall disclosed by letter to Seward his belief based on letters he had received from friends in the South that "there is a combination to prevent the inauguration of the President-elect—even at the peril of his life. What an exposed situation he would be in for 15 minutes on the East Portico!"[4]

Seward, in turn, reported to Lincoln: "I am not giving you opinions and rumors," concerning an assassination plot, before advising him to come to Washington "earlier than you otherwise would" and to do so "by surprise—without announcement."[5]

At the same time, Theodorus Bailey Myers, a New York attorney, warned Harriet Lane, the niece of President Buchanan, of a "powerful clique at work at Washington who seek for a temporary dissolution of the Union with the hope of a reorganization to cure the existing evil."[6]

Naturally, all of the talk of plots and war depressed the city.

"There is no hilarity in the national capital in these times," a correspondent for the *Charleston Mercury* wrote on Christmas morning. That same day a *Baltimore American* reporter in Washington noted a "general gloom and despondency" underscored by an overcast gray sky that "fully corresponded with the feelings of the people."[7]

The ennui was shattered two days later when dispatches arrived in the city from Charleston indicating that Major Robert Anderson, taking stock of what he thought was an indefensible station at Fort Moultrie off the South Carolina coast, had moved his men to the nearby and larger Fort Sumter--in essence trading a weaker position for one stronger.[8]

South Carolinians instantly regarded Anderson's move as an act of aggression challenging their newly independent state. Angrily they proclaimed that they could not abide having a "foreign-occupied" fort in their territory--and one with an obviously better chance of repelling an attack than Fort Moultrie.

Buchanan, too, was not happy with Anderson's actions, but now was confronted with a challenge made by South Carolina commissioners arriving in Washington who demanded that the president order Anderson to remove his men and return to Fort Moultrie.

It had not been Buchanan's original idea to entertain representatives from South Carolina or any other seceded state. Instead he had earlier considered a suggestion made by Supreme Court Associate Justice John Campbell that the federal government should appoint its own commissioners— Campbell specifically recommended Franklin Pierce—to go to the South with the goal of stamping out the secession movement. Now meeting instead with the South Carolina commissioners,

Buchanan was careful to make no commitments, arguing that he first must take matters up with his cabinet.[9]

When he did, he encountered Jeremiah Black, his former attorney general who was now the new Secretary of State; Edwin Stanton, the new attorney general; and Joseph Holt, who was about to become the new Secretary of War. All three men were staunch Unionists and pushed Buchanan to take a strong stand that, while stopping short of openly backing Anderson, still refused to order him back to Fort Moultrie.

On December 31, Buchanan even approved a plan greatly urged by General Scott to send the civilian steamer *Star of the West* to resupply Anderson's forces with food and reinforcements (the ship would eventually be forced to retreat to the North after being fired upon in South Carolina).

On New Year's Day John Tyler offered one of the few positive reviews of Buchanan's handling of the secession crisis, noting simply: "The President pursues a wise and statesmanlike course."

There were many reasons why Tyler, almost alone among both Northern and Southern political leaders, would find anything good to say about Buchanan. Tyler's sons, Robert and John, Jr., had been prominent backers of Buchanan for more than two decades; with Robert, as the chairman of the Pennsylvania Democratic party, having a vested interest in Buchanan's success. As president, Buchanan returned the favor by keeping the White House doors opened to practically the entire Tyler clan.

But Tyler might have most sympathized with Buchanan because he, too, had endured a presidential crisis in 1841 when he twice vetoed bills to create a national bank, and by so doing saw almost his entire cabinet resign in protest.

In his post-presidential years Tyler continued to regard himself—and was so viewed by many others—as a renegade. At the same time, in the manner of a well-bred Virginian, he believed that almost anything could be accomplished if and when gentlemen came together to discuss their differences.

"I have for some time thought that a conference between the Border slaveholding and non-slaveholding states would result in harmony," Tyler confided to David Gardiner.[10]

Tyler got his chance to prove his theory two weeks later when Virginia lawmakers debated a bill, inspired by a public letter Tyler had written to the *Richmond Enquirer*, calling for a "peace convention" that would be attended by both Northern and Southern representatives. The legislature appointed the former president to head up the effort.[11]

Tyler was initially unenthused. He thought someone younger should take the assignment and was additionally put off that lawmakers had enlarged his original border state proposal to include all of the states of the Union, arguing that if the Southern states most likely to secede boycotted what was now referred to as the Peace Conference, the proceedings would end up being dominated by the North.

Despite his reservations, Tyler agreed to serve. His timing, from the perspective of Southerners who still wanted to stay in the Union, could not have been better. By the time that Tyler on January 23 arrived in Washington where the deliberations for the conference would be held, four more states had seceded: Mississippi on January 2, Florida on January 10, Alabama on January 11 and Georgia on January 19.

On January 20, Jefferson Davis, in Washington, wrote a heart-felt letter to his old friend Franklin Pierce, announcing

"I leave immediately for Mississippi and know not what may devolve upon me after my return."[12]

Davis had finally decided to end his relationship with both the Senate and the Union. His disappointment in the failure of the Committee of Thirteen to present a workable anti-secession compromise plan made it impossible for him to remain in the Union. Nor was Davis alone in his despair: in New York, former president Martin Van Buren noted that Davis had been more than willing to "accept Mr. Crittenden's proposition as a final settlement of the controversy, if tendered & sustained by the Republican members."

But it was the Republicans who refused to bend, noted Van Buren, as he wondered if the country really appreciated the "full measure of their [the Republicans] responsibility" in destroying the Crittenden compromise.[13]

"We recur to the principles upon which our government was founded," Davis said during his dramatic farewell remarks on January 21, "and when you deny them, and when you deny us the right to withdraw from a government which thus perverted threatens to be destructive of our rights, we but tread in the path of our fathers when we proclaim our independence and take the hazard."[14]

The Republican hard line was most prominently argued by Seward who, until Lincoln made it to Washington, was the most important Republican in the city. When his son Frederick, who would serve as assistant secretary of state, arrived in Washington on January 29, he noted that his father "Is overwhelmed with letters & visitors imploring him to save the Union" and is "the only person who appears to be entirely patient with each, unconverted by any, and confident, cheerful & happy about the result."[15]

Like Seward, Tyler was also becoming the center of his own universe.

He would meet with Buchanan several times over the course of the next few weeks, at one point observing of the president: "His policy is obviously to throw all responsibility off his shoulders." As the other members of the Peace Convention, which would include James Guthrie of Kentucky, Salmon Chase (soon to be Lincoln's Treasury Secretary) of Ohio, prominent businessman Erastus Corning of New York, and Andrew Johnson pal Samuel Milligan of Tennessee, among more than 130 delegates, arrived in Washington, Tyler's young wife Julia Gardiner Tyler wondered: "Perhaps I am here during the last days of the Republic."[16]

If so, Mrs. Tyler admitted that she thought it was all terribly exciting. She was particularly taken with the gallant impression has husband made. The *New York Tribune* observed that the former president "Bears his age with remarkable grace; he is still the same slim, tall-looking, high-bred Virginia gentleman, his striking features still showing a high degree of mental activity."[17]

On February 3, Mrs. Tyler noted that her husband "has been surrounded with visitors from the moment he could appear to them...they are all looking to him in the settlement of the vexed question. His superiority over everybody else is felt and admitted by all."[18]

Meeting in the concert hall of the Willard Hotel, the Peace Convention heard a hopeful Tyler declare: "If you reach the height of this great occasion, your children's children will rise up and call you blessed."[19]

Yet, from the start, Tyler also knew that the obstacles before the convention were great, and not just because it's mission was the gigantic one of stopping secession and war. Tyler was also confronted with a membership that did not present a balanced picture of the country: the pro-secession Deep South states did not even bother to send representatives. Several Northern states, too, were no-shows, and of the ones that did send delegates there was a tendency to reject any proposal that in even the smallest fashion acknowledged the South's issues.

The convention's public relations took a hit when it was decided that all proceedings should be off-limits to the press. "The citizens are indignant that the meetings should be held in a small hall with closed doors," complained a *New York Herald* reporter on February 4, the opening day of the gathering. "It is regarded more as a dark lantern convention than one to whose deliberations the largest publicity should be given."[20]

Tyler was also hamstrung by the fact that delegates to the convention took a long time getting there: Maine and Massachusetts were not represented until February 9, while those already in attendance were derided for being mostly older men many years out of public life who liked to give long speeches. "They are the fossil remains of another generation, brought to the surface again by the storm of secession," noted the *New York Herald* reporter, perhaps still miffed that he was not privy to the proceedings.[21]

The Peace Convention particularly suffered in comparison to the energy and excitement surrounding the opening, also on February 4, of the convention of seceded states gathering in the main meeting hall of the State House in Montgomery, Alabama.

A town of just under 9,000 people, Montgomery was muddy and wet from a recent downpour, yet excited over the prospects of not only hosting the historic conference, but hopefully becoming the official capital for the seceded states. "Our Montgomery people don't do things by halves," one local boaster would declare as Montgomery's leaders set out to convince delegates from the seceded states to set up permanent headquarters in the city.[22]

Until that decision was made, Montgomery residents could look on in awe as any number of well-known Southern leaders and agitators passed through the elegant marble-columned entrance to the Alabama statehouse: state-home favorite William Yancey, at long last seeing his vision of a Southern nation becoming a reality; the thoughtful and skeptical Alexander Stephens of Georgia; South Carolina fire-eater Robert Barnwell Rhett, Sr.; and the hard-drinking and loud Robert Tombs, recently a U.S. Senator from Georgia.

But probably the most prominent man in Montgomery was Howell Cobb, who had only two months earlier resigned as Buchanan's Treasury Secretary and now had every reason to believe that he was going to be, based on his fame and popularity, the first president of the new confederacy. For now, Cobb would have to settle for the presidency of the convention itself, elected by acclamation on the first day of the proceedings and setting a humorous and rebellious note when he declared in a twist on Andrew Johnson's argument that being a part of the Union was a perpetual commitment: "It's now a fact, irrevocable fact—the separation is perfect, complete and perpetual."[23]

By the time of the Montgomery convention, Jefferson Davis was already back in Mississippi where he learned that Governor John Pettus had commissioned him as a major general of the Army of Mississippi. Davis was delighted with the position, but quickly pointed out to state leaders the seriousness of the situation, the increasing likelihood of war and the need for more arms. From there he and Varina and their three children went to the family plantation in Brierfield.

Several days later Davis received startling news: the confederates meeting in Montgomery had by-passed Cobb in favor of electing the Mississippian as the Provisional President of the Confederate States of America. The vice-presidential nod was given to Stephens.

In Montgomery the selection was greeted with fireworks and canon fire. At Brierfield it was met with silence as Davis contemplated taking a job he had no interest in holding.

With the Montgomery delegates also swiftly approving a provisional constitution modeled after the U.S. Constitution, all was ready for the expected arrival of Davis on February 16. As Davis quickly prepared for a trip that would take him from Jackson to Chattanooga to Atlanta and, finally, to Montgomery—traveling nearly 700 miles to a city that was actually only 200 miles from Jackson (a sign of the chaotic Southern rail system), Abraham Lincoln was saying goodbye to his neighbors in Springfield, about to embark upon one of the most publicized journeys in American political history.

More than a thousand people gathered around the town's Western Railroad Depot as Lincoln, his wife Mary and two of their younger boys, said goodbye. For Lincoln, a man not given to public displays of emotion, it was a sentimental moment.

"No one in my position can appreciate the sadness I feel at this parting," he began. "To this place and the kindness of these people, I owe everything. Here I have lived a quarter of a century, and have passed from a young man to an old man. Here my children have been born, and one is buried."

"I now leave," Lincoln added, "not knowing when, or whether ever, I may return, with a task before me greater than that which rested upon Washington."[24]

As the presidential caravan headed towards Indianapolis, Lincoln was aware that all of his public words were being recorded by the national press and determined that his remarks should somehow present a balance between downplaying secession and bolstering the spirits of the Union. Accordingly, in Indianapolis, where he was greeted by a 34-gun salute and a parade composed of local political and military officials, Lincoln seemed to be speaking directly to Jefferson Davis when he talked about the concepts of coercion and invasion.

"What is the meaning of these words?" Lincoln asked. "Would marching an army into South Carolina with hostile attempt be an invasion? I think it would, and would be coercion if the South Carolinians are forced to submit."

"But," Lincoln continued, "if the United States should merely hold and retake its own forts, collect duties or withhold mail facilities where habitually violated, would any or all of these things be invasion or coercion? Do professional Union lovers, resolved to resist coercion, understand such things? If they do, their idea is light and airy."

"In their view, the Union, as a family relation, would seem no regular marriage, but a sort of free love arrangement to be maintained by personal attraction," Lincoln added to laughter and cheers.[25]

While Lincoln was still in Indiana, Davis was met with a highly enthusiastic crowd at the depot in Jackson. Inside the state capital, where he was repeatedly cheered, Davis was in a bellicose mood, declaring that if was to be a civil war, the fighting "will be upon Northern soil and not upon Southern."

If the North provoked the fight, Davis added, he was for "carrying it into their midst."

"Make them support the contending armies and endure the evils of civil war," Davis challenged.[26]

On February 13, Lincoln and his party made it to Columbus where he was again greeted by a lively crowd and colorful military escort. It was here that word arrived of the official voting of the electoral college in Washington—an event that went off without incident despite the worries of Scott and Seward who were convinced that secessionists would disrupt the proceedings. Stops in Cleveland and a half dozen small towns in western Ohio preceded Lincoln's arrival in Buffalo on February 16 where more than 10,000 were waiting to cheer him.

Buffalo proved a scary visit. Greeted at the station by Millard Fillmore, who warmly shook hands with the president-elect, Lincoln was instantly mobbed by onlookers and only with difficulty was escorted to that city's American Hotel where, facing yet another group of people that closed in around him, broke free and delivered a brief address declaring his fealty to state's rights and the constitution.

The following morning Fillmore arrived by carriage outside the hotel, escorting Lincoln to a nearby Unitarian church. After the service was over, and now joined by Mary, Lincoln was treated to lunch at Fillmore's comfortable downtown mansion. Buffalo Republicans who might have been angry that Lincoln spent most of the afternoon with the former president were instead pleased that Fillmore seemed to be so supportive. A *New York Herald* reporter talking to local residents telegraphed on February 17: "The marked courtesy of Mr. Fillmore to the president-elect was the subject of general praise today."[27]

As Fillmore bade the Lincolns farewell, Davis was on the last leg of his journey, finally arriving in Montgomery. From the balcony of the Exchange Hotel Davis later told a late-night crowd: "For now we are brethren, not in name merely, but in fact, men of one flesh, one bone, one interest, one purpose and of an identity of democratic institutions."

Like Lincoln, Davis tried to strike a confident note. But unlike Lincoln, he made it clear that the Union was no longer what it had been. Noting that the day in Montgomery had started out with rain but ended up sunny, and perhaps unintentionally revealing his own stark appraisal of current conditions, he added "So will the progress of the Southern Confederacy carry us safe to the harbor of constitutional liberty and political equality."[28]

Davis promised to have much more to say during his inaugural address the following day, on February 18.

As Davis finally rested, Lincoln was already in Albany on the way to what was expected to be a massive and unprecedented reception in New York City.

He was by this time feeling the burden of the long journey and endless demand to give a speech in every town. His throat was sore and he felt sick. But responding to large and friendly crowds in Hudson, Poughkeepsie and Peekskill, Lincoln made brief remarks, riding into New York City by late afternoon where he and Mary and the boys were escorted to the elegant Astor House, waving on the way to a crowd in excess of 250,000.

That evening Lincoln spoke briefly before a group of well-heeled New York Republicans, but declined to offer any specifics regarding the direction of his administration. "I have kept silence for the reason that I supposed it was peculiarly proper that I should do so until the time came when, according to the customs of the country, I should speak officially," Lincoln remarked, drawing a jeer from at least one member of the audience.[29]

The following morning Lincoln had breakfast with a group of Wall Street businessmen and investors who did not seem particularly enthusiastic about meeting him, and then traveled to City Hall where Mayor Fernando Wood, who had earlier aired a plan for New York City to secede, conspicuously told Lincoln that New Yorkers were looking for a "restoration of fraternal relations between the states—only to be accomplished by peaceful and conciliatory means."[30]

In response, Lincoln candidly admitted that the vast majority of New York City voters had cast their ballots against him in the November election, and then smartly said he agreed with Wood's sentiments, likening the United States to a ship and New York City to its cargo: "I understand the ship to be made for the carrying and preservation of the cargo, and so long as the ship can be saved with the cargo, it should never be abandoned."[31]

By the time of Lincoln's arrival in New York, all of the city's major newspapers had given extensive coverage to the inauguration of Jefferson Davis, described by the *New York Times* as the "greatest pageant ever witnessed in the South."[32]

In his speech, Davis cleverly sought to align the spirit of the new Confederacy with the American revolution, noting "Our present condition, achieved in a manner unprecedented in the history of nations, illustrates the American idea that government rests upon the consent of the governed, and that it is right for the people to alter and abolish governments whenever they become destructive to the ends for which they were established."

Davis pointedly noted that the creation of the Confederacy "has been marked by no aggression upon others, and followed by no domestic convulsions." The new nation, he said, only wanted to exist alongside the Union in peace. He added that if the United States should pursue war "the suffering of millions will bear testimony to the policy and wickedness of our aggressors."

Davis concluded by candidly suggesting his leadership would "see many errors to forgive, many deficiencies to tolerate," but that he would not be lacking in "zeal or fidelity to the cause that is to me the highest in hope and of most enduring affection."[33]

After the extensive all-day ceremonies, Davis hosted a reception at the nearby Estelle Hall. Fireworks sounded and bands played late into the evening.

Lincoln and his party left New York on February 21, traveling through New Jersey and stopping for a brief speech in Trenton before arriving late in the afternoon in Philadelphia. That evening the president-elect was told of a plot to assassinate him when he arrived in Baltimore. Allen Pinkerton, the head of the Pinkerton National Detective Agency, was convinced that there were plans afoot to shoot Lincoln as he left the Calvert Street Station in that city and rode to the Camden Street Station for the final leg of his journey to Washington. Pinkerton's advice was nearly identical to the advice Seward gave Lincoln in late December: he should come to Washington ahead of schedule, and by so doing go through Baltimore immediately on a night train.[34]

As he did with Seward, Lincoln rejected Pinkerton's advice, insisting that he must appear the next day at Independence Hall in Philadelphia and, later, at the Pennsylvania statehouse in Harrisburg.

Lincoln kept those commitments, but on the night of February 22 received written information handed to him by Frederick Seward which contained memos compiled by William Seward and General Scott providing additional details on Baltimore. "After a few words of friendly greeting with inquiries about my father and matters in Washington, he sat down by the table under the gas-light to peruse the letter I had brought," young Seward later recalled.[35]

Lincoln promised to give the matter serious consideration. The next day he reluctantly agreed to alter his travel plans. Mary and the boys, not familiar to the public, would go ahead as previously planned, while Lincoln—along with Pinkerton—quietly boarded a late evening train to Baltimore from Philadelphia. Arriving around 3 a.m., he boarded a separate train to Washington where he was then driven to the Willard Hotel.

The stealthy nocturnal journey proved to be a rare strategic mistake for Lincoln, opening him up to ridicule in the national press. The *New York Times* only made things worse when it reported that Lincoln was wearing a Scotch plaid cap and long military coat on the journey, which fed the imagination of cartoonists—one for *Vanity Fair* would show Lincoln prancing in a plaid Scottish kilt and fetching feathered beret.

Even those who admired Lincoln regretted the strange ending to his grand journey. William Schley, a Lincoln supporter in Baltimore, acknowledged that the president-elect's life could well have been in danger in that city. Nevertheless he described to Lincoln the "disappointment at the announcement of your 'passage' through unseen, unnoticed and unknown—it fell like a thunderclap upon the community."[36]

John Harper, a Lincoln man and business associate of Schuyler Colfax in Indiana, began a letter to Colfax: "I am happy to find that Old Abe has landed safely at the Capital, yet I don't know what I should have rather seen him gone in on the train he was expected to come in on."[37]

Despite the controversy, Lincoln was at last in Washington, where he would be joined by Mary and the boys who would arrive safely later that same day

CHAPTER SEVEN ENDNOTES

[1]William Pennington to Zachariah Chandler, 22 December 1860, Papers of Zachariah Chandler, Reel 1.

[2]Winfield Scott, *Memoirs of Lieut. General Scott—Volume II* (New York: Sheldon and Company, 1864), 611-612.

[3]Ibid.

[4]"From Washington," *Springfield Daily Republican,* 4 January 1861, p. 2; Abram Randall to William Seward, 15 December 1860, Abraham Lincoln Papers, Reel 12.

[5]William Seward to Abraham Lincoln, 29 December 1860, Abraham Lincoln Papers, Reel 12.

[6]Theodorus Bailey Myers to Harriet Lane, 28 December 1860, Papers of James Buchanan and Harriet L. Johnston, Reel 3.

[7]"Gossip from the Federal Capital," *Charleston Mercury,* 29 December 1860, p. 4; "Letter from Washington," *Baltimore American,* 28 December 1860, p. 1.

[8]"Highly Important," *New York Tribune,* 31 December 1860, p. 5; "Major Anderson's Coup d' Etat," *Springfield Daily Republican,* 31 December 1860, p. 2.

[9]John Campbell to Franklin Pierce, 19 December 1860, Franklin Pierce Papers, Series 3, Reel 2.

[10]Lyon G. Tyler, *The Letters and Times of the Tylers—Volume II* (New York: Da Capo Press, 1970), 578.

[11]Ibid.

[12]Jefferson Davis to Franklin Pierce, 20 December 1860, Franklin Pierce Papers, Series 3, Reel 2.

[13]Martin Van Buren speech draft, uncertain date, most likely spring 1860, Martin Van Buren Papers, Reel 34, Series 2.

[14]*Congressional Globe, 2nd Session, 36th Congress* (Washington: John C. Rives Publishing, 1861), 487.

[15]Frederick Seward to Frances Seward, 30 January 1860, Seward Family Papers, Reel 118.

[16]Tyler, *The Letters and Times of the Tylers,* 590; Julia Gardiner Tyler to Juliana Gardiner, 3 February 1861, John Tyler Papers, Reel 2, Series 1.

[17]"From Virginia," *New York Tribune,* 26 January 1861, p. 6.

[18]Julia Gardiner Tyler to Juliana Gardiner, 3 February 1861, John Tyler Papers, Reel 2, Series 1.

[19]Allen Nivens, *The Emergence of Lincoln* (New York: Charles Scribner's Sons, 1950), 412.

[20]"The Revolution," *New York Herald*, 5 February 1861, p.1.

[21]There were indications that more than a few of the Northern delegates had little interest in seeing the Peace Conference succeed. In Michigan, the powerful Zachariah Chandler suggesting sending "stiff-backed men or none" to the convention, adding that "the whole thing was gotten up against my judgment and will end in thin smoke." "The Peace Convention at Washington," *New York Herald*, p. 1; "To the Voters of Michigan," early February 1861, Papers of Zachariah Chandler, Reel 1.

[22] William C. Davis, *A Government of Our Own—The Making of the Confederacy* (New York: The Free Press, 1994), 146.

[23]"Important from the South," *New York Herald*, 9 February 1861, p. 10.

[24]Even before Lincoln's departure, Thaddeus Stevens was worried that the prominence of the strong-willed William Seward and Simon Cameron in the up-coming cabinet would make it almost impossible for Lincoln to govern once he finally did become president: "Will Lincoln have the nerve to resist," Stevens asked Salmon Chase on February 3. "Will he have a cabinet who will resist?" "Mr. Lincoln's Farewell to His Neighbors," *Springfield Daily Republican*, 12

February 1861, p. 4; "The President Elect En Route," *New York Tribune*, 12 February 1861, p. 5; Thaddeus Stevens to Salmon Chase, 3 February 1861, Thaddeus Stevens Papers, Series 1, Reel 2.

[25]"Progress of the President-Elect," *Baltimore American*, 14 February 1861, p. 1.

[26]"Reception of Gen. Jeff Davis at Jackson, Mississippi," *Louisville Daily Courier*, 18 February 1861, p. 1.

[27]"Reception and Speech at Buffalo," *New York Times*, 18 February 1861, p. 1; "Movements of Mr. Lincoln," *New York Herald*, 18 February 1861, p. 4.

[28]"The National Crisis," *New York Herald*, 18 February 1861, p. 1; "From Montgomery," *Charleston Mercury*, 18 February 1861, p. 3.

[29]"The Presidential Progress," *New York Herald*, 20 February 1860, p. 1.

[30]"Lincoln and Hamlin in New York," *New York Tribune*, 21 February 1861, p. 8.

[31]. Ibid.

[32]"Important from Montgomery," *New York Times*, 19 February 1861, p. 8.

[33]"Jeff Davis at Montgomery," *Louisville Daily Courier*, 19 February 1861, p. 3.

[34]William Seward to Abraham Lincoln, 21 February 1861, Abraham Lincoln Papers, Reel 17.

[35]Doris Kearns Goodwin, *Team of Rivals—The Political Genius of Abraham Lincoln* (New York: Simon & Schuster, 2005), 311.

[36]William Schley to Abraham Lincoln, 19 February 1861, Abraham Lincoln Papers, Reel 17.

[37]John Harper to Schuyler Colfax, 25 February 1861, Papers of Schuyler Colfax, 25 February 1861.

CHAPTER EIGHT

———

"No Time for Effective Assemblages of the People."

As Lincoln was ushered to his suite at the Willard Hotel, the delegates to John Tyler's Peace Conference were getting ready to hold yet another tiring day-long session.

Tyler was weary. Not only were his worst fears about Northern and Southern delegates refusing to compromise becoming a reality, but President Buchanan would not leave him alone. Repeatedly since Tyler's arrival in Washington, Buchanan had requested his presence at the White House or simply dropped in on Tyler at the Willard.

Buchanan obviously turned to Tyler because Tyler was the stronger man: resolute, firm and not given to endless uncertainty, all qualities that Buchanan lacked.

And it wasn't just that Buchanan wanted to know how the Peace Conference was proceeding. He also asked Tyler to use his influence in Charleston and Montgomery to find out whether it was true that a Confederate attack on Fort Sumter was in the making. Promptly Tyler wrote to Jefferson Davis who assured him that no such action was contemplated.

But sometimes much more mundane matters struck Buchanan as being worthy of a visit to Tyler. On February 21, the president stopped by Tyler's room and not finding him there penned a quick note: "I called to see you this evening to consult you about a matter of some little importance," Buchanan began, adding "Ought the federal troops now in Washington to parade tomorrow with the local volunteers. I thought if this were done it might arouse the susceptibilities of Southern members of the Peace Convention."[1]

In response, Tyler advised the president to cancel the parade. And in almost classic Buchanan fashion, he did as Tyler suggested, then quickly rescinded his own order once he learned, on the day of the event, that it angered Washington parade-goers.

After the Peace Conference adjourned on the evening of February 23, Tyler and a majority of the delegates decided to make a courtesy call on Lincoln. Following a cordial exchange of greetings, the men engaged in a remarkably frank discussion. Southern delegates told the president-elect that the North was the most to blame for the current crisis. At the same time a Pennsylvania delegate advised that the only course available was one of compromise.

To the first charge, Lincoln forcefully contended that the North had in fact behaved with restraint, even going so far as to enforce Fugitive Slave Laws which it found offensive. To the second, Lincoln responded: "If I remember correctly, *that* is not what *I* was elected for."[2]

Reporters naturally wondered what effect Lincoln's presence and words might have on the Northern delegates. Tyler quietly hoped a well-timed signal from the president-elect might result in a more conciliatory attitude among those delegates, which might spark a positive Southern response. But in fact, Lincoln urged the Northerners to hang tough, making Tyler's task nearly impossible.

The last meeting of the Peace Conference was held on February 27 with members officially voting to send an uneven series of proposals for holding off the crisis to Congress. Tyler regarded the group's final recommendations as weak, but reporters noted that the Southern delegates did come up with one tangible solution to the question of slavery being extended into the territories: if it was a problem, the US should simply stop expanding, they suggested.

Exhausted, Tyler offered his blessings to the Peace Conference's final resolutions, declaring "God protect our country and the Union of these states, which was committed to us as the blood-bought legacy of our heroic ancestors." A *Richmond Dispatch* correspondent, reading the conference recommendations, predicted that upon close examination Congress would easily pick up on the "Hollowness and insubstantiality of the whole affair."[3]

The recommendations, in fact, went nowhere in Congress. Both Northern Democrats and Republicans, for different reasons, ignored them. The House actually voted to not even officially receive the document. In the Senate things were hardly better. John Crittenden of Kentucky, already wise in the way of failed compromises, offered the Peace Conference's recommendations as his own, only to see his bill rejected 28 to 7. Virginia Senator James Mason, in a letter to Tyler on

March 2, contended that legislators from the two sections of the country were simply no longer capable of even trying to understand each other, noting that some Northerners thought they could make things right by simply opposing any constitutional amendment giving Congress power over slavery in the states. It was an idea that Mason described as a "miserable evasion."

"What a commentary on what these gentlemen take to be the position of our honored state," Mason added.[4]

By the time he had received Mason's letter, Tyler had returned to Virginia where he had been elected to serve in a state convention considering secession. Although he had been charmed by Lincoln's candor at the Willard Hotel meeting, Tyler had become more convinced than ever that the unity of the nation was a thing of the past. Learning of the Peace Conference recommendations' sad fate in Congress, Tyler came to a profound conclusion considering that he had once been a United States president: the South was right to secede and Virginia should join the cause.

Next to Jefferson Davis, Tyler was the most prominent American in the winter of 1861 to not only advocate secession, but personally participate in it. As Congress neared adjournment, also on March 2, Speaker of the House William Pennington took note of a significantly reduced membership. Virtually all of the representatives from the seceded states were gone, and the same was true in the Senate. Departing with tradition, Pennington stepped down from the Speaker's chair so that he could talk from the floor, where he declared that while he would miss those Southerners who had departed, he remained convinced that "No tenable ground has been assigned for a dissolution of the ties which binded every

American citizen to his country—and impartial history will so decide."[5]

In the busy days after his meeting with Tyler and the Peace Conference members, Lincoln familiarized himself with Washington. With William Seward invariably at his side, he visited both Congress and the Supreme Court and attended several parties with Mary. In what free time was left, Lincoln finalized his cabinet picks and worked on his all-important inaugural address, going back and forth over it with Seward, who generally suggested a more conciliatory theme.

In the White House, Buchanan prepared to leave. He had sent a request to Congress asking for more troops to help secure the Capitol on inaugural day, but denied that he himself was nervous. "I shall ride beside Mr. Lincoln from the White House to the Capitol, even if it rains bullets," Buchanan declared.[6]

On the night before the inaugural, Washington was alive with anticipation. Reporters estimated that up to 100,000 visitors had arrived to witness Lincoln's swearing-in. All of the city's hotels were full, forcing many out-of-towners to sleep where they could, sitting up on chairs in taverns and, for a lucky few, in the corridors of the Capitol.[7]

By morning, soldiers under the direct order of Winfield Scott took up positions on buildings along the parade route as Buchanan and Lincoln left the Willard in an open carriage.

Waving to enthused crowds on both sides of Pennsylvania Avenue, the two men were part of a lengthy colorful parade that included a military escort, several bands, some 400 Republican campaign workers, aged veterans of the Revolutionary War, and what was particularly remarked upon by the correspondent for the *Charleston Mercury*: "A large car, draped and festooned, and filled with little children." Waving miniature flags, each child represented one of the states of the union—before secession.[8]

Inside the Senate chamber John Breckinridge swore in Hannibal Hamlin as the new vice-president. "At ten minutes after 1 o'clock an unusual stir occurred in the chamber, and the rumor spread that the President-elect was in the building," noted a reporter for the *New York Tribune*, giving his readers a minute-by-minute account of the day's proceedings.[9]

That excitement reached a crescendo as Lincoln walked out onto a hastily-built wooden platform on the east portico of the Capitol. Members of Congress who had spent the last session heatedly arguing over the fate of the nation now applauded as Lincoln moved to the podium overlooking a crowd of some 30,000 people. Taking off his hat, Lincoln looked around for a place to put it. Stephen Douglas jumped quickly to his side, remarking "Permit me, sir," as he grabbed Lincoln's topper.[10]

Pulling out a pair of steel-rimmed spectacles from his breast pocket, which surprised some in the crowd who didn't know that Lincoln needed reading glasses, he began his address, a speech that emphatically asserted that his accession to the presidency was no cause for alarm.

"Indeed, the most ample evidence to the contrary has all the while existed," Lincoln argued, quoting from earlier remarks he had made in which he declared "I have no purpose, directly or indirectly, to interfere with the institution of slavery where it exists. I believe I have no lawful right to do so, and I have no inclination to do so."

"Those who nominated and elected me did so with full knowledge that I had made this and many similar declarations and had never recanted them," Lincoln continued.

But after offering a lengthy examination of the constitutional relationship between the states and the federal government, Lincoln left no doubt as to where he stood regarding secession: "Plainly, the central idea of secession is the essence of anarchy. A majority held in restraint by constitutional checks and limitations, and always changing easily with deliberate changes of popular opinions and sentiments, is the only true sovereign of a free people. Whoever rejects it does, of necessity, fly to anarchy or despotism. Unanimity is impossible; the rule of a minority, as a permanent arrangement, is wholly inadmissible; so that rejecting the majority principle, anarchy or despotism in some form is all that is left."

Finally arguing that the ultimate fate, along with what he described as the "momentous issue of civil war," was in the hands of the people, Lincoln closed with a paragraph he had greatly improved upon after suggestions from Seward: "We are not enemies, but friends. We must not be enemies. Though passion may have strained, it must not break our bonds of affection. The mystic chords of memory, stretching from every battlefield and patriot grave to every living heart and hearthstone all over this broad land, will yet swell the chorus of the Union when again touched, as surely they will be, by the better angels of our nature."[11]

Upon concluding his speech, Lincoln was most conspicuously congratulated by Douglas, who throughout the address had been heard several times to comment "Good," or "That's so." Buchanan, who had looked down on his boots throughout most of the address, told a reporter that he could not "understand the secret meaning" of the speech and would have more to say after reading it later for himself. Winfield Scott, who was not within hearing distance of the speech, but stood with his solders near the Capitol grounds, was simply relieved that Lincoln had gotten through the ceremony alive, exclaiming "God be praised," when he learned that Lincoln had concluded his remarks.[12]

It was hard at first to gauge the public response to Lincoln's speech. "We are waiting to hear how the country receives the Inaugural and Cabinet," Frederick Seward wrote several days later. "Washington affords very little reliable indication. It is all Republican now as it was all Democratic two months ago."[13]

Most Southern newspapers condemned the address, but individual Southerners were less critical. "I can't see anything warlike in Mr. Lincoln's Inaugural," Alabama businessman Joseph Bradley wrote Andrew Johnson on March 8, before adding: "If Lincoln will only remain inactive--& make no attempts to repossess the forts—south--the conservative feeling in the seceding states will react."[14]

That, of course, was the precise challenge facing Lincoln on his first full day in office. Meeting with Scott, Lincoln discussed a new report communicated by Major Robert Anderson indicating that without reinforcements, Fort Sumter would have to be abandoned by mid-April. In response, Scott did not see how enough men could be gotten together to help the situation and so told Lincoln. Several days later, in answer to a written request from Lincoln, Scott estimated that Anderson had "hard bread, flour & rice for about 26 days," but added that to reinforce him would require "a fleet of vessels and transports," and several thousand troops.[15]

Lincoln, who had come to like Scott's blunt manner, must have been depressed by the General's appraisal.

Seward now weighed in on Fort Sumter: In response to a general query that Lincoln also sent to the other members of the cabinet, the Secretary of State argued against reinforcing the fort, if it could only be done with a military force, because such a force would "provoke combat and probably initiate a civil war."[16]

Seward's assessment was shared by Secretary of War Simon Cameron, Secretary of the Navy Gideon Welles, Attorney General Edward Bates and Secretary of the Interior Caleb Smith. Postmaster General Montgomery Blair was for reinforcement, as was Secretary of the Treasury Salmon Chase, on the theory that it was "highly improbable" that such an action would inflame the South to the point of starting a war.[17]

In Montgomery, the members of Jefferson Davis's cabinet were all in place by the time of Lincoln's inaugural, and like their Washington counterparts, daily trying to develop a coherent strategy regarding Fort Sumter. One thing was certain, according to a *Baltimore American* reporter in Montgomery familiar with the new government's thinking: some kind of military action was inevitable. "South Carolina will have the honor of firing the first gun. Alabama and Florida the next— Sumter must fall." Quoting friends of Davis, the reporter added that after Sumter was captured, the battle would be "carried into Africa"--otherwise known as the North.[18]

There were actually few indications that Davis himself was feeling so belligerent. On the contrary, overwhelmed with his duties as the chief executive of a one-month old nation, Davis was hopeful that Lincoln would simply abandon Fort Sumter.

But by sending commissioners to Washington, Davis soon learned that the Lincoln administration had no intention of bargaining over anything, much less Sumter (although Seward had seemed to hold out some hope for a compromise). At the same time, Davis had sent his brigadier general, the strong-willed Pierre G. T. Beauregard, to Charleston to block any federal reinforcements from getting to Sumter and additionally made it known that he supported the construction of batteries around Charleston. Yet it was Davis who soon came to regard Washington as the aggressive party, informing South Carolina Governor Francis Pickens on March 18 that it was improbable that "the enemy would retire peacefully from your harbor."[19]

Publicly Davis sought to portray the Confederacy as merely trying to go about its own business, harboring no ill will towards the North. Colonel Ambrose Dudley Mann, obviously improvising on the Confederate party line, even went so far as to tell a *New York Herald* reporter that the Confederate government possessed "none other than the most friendly feelings and are extremely desirous of cultivating the kindest relations" with the North. The reporter added that the government in Montgomery would "do all in their power to prevent the shedding of blood."[20]

Davis finally got a clear signal from Washington on March 29 when Lincoln announced that the federal government would not only not evacuate Fort Sumter but would send a force to support and supply Anderson and his men. Perhaps unwilling to recognize the inevitable, Davis continued to hope that "for political reasons, the U.S. Gov't will avoid making an attack so long as the hope of retaining the border states remains."[21]

As events were clearly speeding towards a confrontation, some newspapers began to blame the nation's former presidents for precipitating the crisis. The *Weekly Wisconsin Patriot* on March 3 lambasted the Fillmore administration for ignoring the "question of extending slavery and all other questions connected with that infamous institution." Several days later the *Morning Oregonian* said it was all the fault of both the Pierce and Buchanan administrations, noting that "For eight years the national government has been too feeble to maintain tranquility at home."[22]

None of the former presidents responded to the attacks. In fact, both Martin Van Buren and Fillmore said they were impressed by Lincoln and declined to criticize him. Tyler, Pierce and Buchanan, the ex-presidents least likely to approve Lincoln's course, for the moment remained quiet.

On April 1 Lincoln asked Winfield Scott to provide him daily reports on military matters. The General's subsequent correspondence revealed how things were coming unraveled.

Noting growing pro-Confederate sympathy in Key West, a strategic outpost vital to Union operations, Scott on April 2 remarked that the island "can only be held & protected for the time by martial law."[23]

On April 5, Scott provided a bleak report on conditions in Washington: "Machinations against the Government & this Capitol are secretly going on all around us—in Virginia, in Maryland & here, as well as further South."[24]

On April 10, Scott noted that Anderson's communications had been severed by South Carolinians, adding "There is an untraceable rumor, in the streets, that some unknown person has received a telegraph stating that the hostile batteries had opened fire" on Fort Sumter.[25]

In fact, on that same day, Beauregard had been given a message by Confederate Secretary of War Leroy Pope Walker ordering him to demand the surrender of Fort Sumter as soon as possible and by so doing effectively preempting any federal move to reinforce it. The next day Beauregard dispatched three messengers to Anderson, telling him to abandon the fort. On April 12, in a subsequent interview with the messengers, Anderson pointed out that if the Confederates could just wait another three days, until April 15, he and his men would be forced to leave Sumter simply because they would have run out of provisions.

This momentarily seemed like a nice way out of the crisis: Anderson and his troops would no longer be in harm's way and the Confederate government would end up in possession of the fort without having fired a single shot, allowing Davis to continue to proclaim that his nation's intentions remained peaceful.

But the three days proved too long for the Confederate government, convinced that during that time Washington could reinforce the fort (in fact, a federal relief fleet arrived on the evening of April 12 and waited just beyond the Charleston harbor hoping to aid Anderson the following morning).

During the second meeting with Anderson, the messengers told him he had just one hour to move out or face Confederate shelling. That firing began in earnest later in the afternoon, ripping into the fort and forcing Anderson to finally withdraw in a dignified ceremony on April 14.

In Charleston and Mercury the streets were quickly filled with cheering people. In the excitement, Secretary Walker brazenly predicted that by May 1 the Confederate flag "would float over the dome of the Old Capitol at Washington." Davis, realizing that the Confederate nation could now expect to be subject to the full wrath of the North, estimated that he would need upwards of 75,000 to 100,000 troops in the field within the next month.[26]

Lincoln was thinking along the same lines. On April 15 he issued an official proclamation calling forth "the militia of the several states of the Union, to the aggregate number of seventy-five thousand." He added: "I deem it proper to say that the first service assigned to the forces hereby called forth will probably be to re-possess the forts."[27]

The Confederate success at Fort Sumter and Lincoln's call to arms brought out Stephen Douglas, who dropped in at the White House and later issued a statement enthusiastically declaring that he was "prepared to fully sustain the President in the exercise of all his constitutional functions, to preserve the Union, maintain the government and defend the capital."[28]

In Richmond, John Tyler was playing a major role in the successful secession vote scheduled to take place on April 17. To his wife, the former president noted "The prospects now are that we shall have war, and a trying one. The battle at Charleston has aroused the whole North. I fear that division no longer exists in their ranks, and that they will break upon the South with an immense force."[29]

In Concord, New Hampshire, Franklin Pierce was beside himself with anxiety. The unleashed fury of the North, he thought, would obviously decimate the South. The fact that his long-time friend Jefferson Davis was at the head of the rebellion targeted for the crushing only made the picture more bleak. Grasping for ideas, Pierce penned a quick letter to Martin Van Buren, wondering if there was "Any human power which can avert the conflict of arms now apparently near at hand, between the two sections of the Union."

Pierce continued: "There is no time for effective assemblages of the people—no time for conventions or discussion." He then proposed that Van Buren, John Tyler, Millard Fillmore and James Buchanan come together in Philadelphia to talk things out, ultimately presenting Lincoln with the result of their collective wisdom.

"Might not their consultation, if it should result in concurrence of judgment, reach the Administration and the country with some degree of power?" Pierced asked.[30]

Pierce additionally suggested that Van Buren should head up the unique effort. In response, Van Buren questioned what such a conference could actually accomplish at such a late date and politely but distinctly suggested that because Pierce obviously had "more hopeful expectations," he should head up the group. It was an idea that Pierce, given his well-known reputation as a pro-Southern man of the North, wisely rejected.[31]

By the time of Van Buren's letter, it had been five days since Lincoln had signed his proclamation. Nothing could be done to turn things around now: no more conventions or compromises or Congressional committees could prevent or postpone the onward march to conflict. All political solutions were at an end: the great Civil War, the tragic consequence of the ascension of Abraham Lincoln, had finally begun.

CHAPTER EIGHT ENDNOTES

[1]James Buchanan to John Tyler, 21 February 1861, John Tyler Papers, Reel 2, Series 1.

[2]Harold Holzer, *Lincoln President-Elect—Abraham Lincoln and the Great Secession Winter, 1860-1861* (New York: Simon & Schuster, 2008), 413-16.

[3]Carl Sandburg, *Abraham Lincoln—The War Years, Volume I* (New York: Harcourt, Brace and Company, 1939), 87-90; "From Washington," *Richmond Dispatch,* 2 March 1861, p. 2.

[4]James Mason to John Tyler, 2 March 1861, John Tyler Papers, Reel 2, Series 1.

[5]*Congressional Globe--2nd Session, 36th Congress,* 1432-33.

[6]"What Mr. Buchanan Proposes to do After the Fourth of March," *Richmond Dispatch*, 4 March 1861, p. 1.

[7]"Inauguration of Abraham Lincoln and Hannibal Hamlin," *Baltimore American,* 5 March 1861, p. 1; "The Day Before the Inauguration," *Springfield Daily Republican*, 5 March 1861, p. 2.

[8]"Our Washington Correspondent," *Charleston Mercury*, 7 March 1861, p. 1.

[9]"The New Administration," *New York Tribune*, 5 March 1861, p. 5.

[10]"Douglas Holding Mr. Lincoln's Hat," *Springfield Daily Republican*, 14 March 1861, p. 2.

[11]Abraham Lincoln 1861 Inaugural Speech, 4 March 1861, Abraham Lincoln Papers, Reel 18.

[12]"The Presidential Inauguration," *Springfield Daily Republican*, 6 March 1861, p. 2.

[13]Frederick Seward to Frances Seward, 6 March 1861, Seward Family Papers, Reel 116.

[14]Joseph Bradley to Andrew Johnson, 8 March 1861, Andrew Johnson Papers, Series 1, Reel 2.

[15]Winfield Scott to Abraham Lincoln, 11 March 1861, Abraham Lincoln Papers, Reel 18.

[16]William Seward to Abraham Lincoln, 15 March 1861, Abraham Lincoln Papers, Reel 18.

[17]Roy P. Basler, *The Collected Works of Abraham Lincoln, Volume IV* (New Brunswick: Rutgers University Press, 1953), 284-85.

[18]"The Southern Confederacy," *Baltimore American*, 12 March 1861, p. 1.

[19]John S. Bowman, *The Civil War Almanac* (New York: World Almanac Publications, 1983), 48.

[20]"Friendly Feeling of the Southern Republic Towards the Government," *New York Herald*, 24 March 1861, p. 4.

[21]Lynda Lasswell Crist, *The Papers of Jefferson Davis, Volume 7, 1861* (Baton Rouge: Louisiana State University Press, 1992), 85-87.

[22]"Seward No Better Than Fillmore," *Weekly Wisconsin Patriot,* 30 March 1861, p. 5; "Facts in History," *The Morning Oregonian*, 11 April 1861, p. 2.

[23]Winfield Scott to Abraham Lincoln, 2 April 1861, Abraham Lincoln Papers, Reel 20.

[24]Winfield Scott to Abraham Lincoln, 5 April 1861, Abraham Lincoln Papers, Reel 20.

[25]Winfield Scott to Abraham Lincoln, 10 April 1861, Abraham Lincoln Papers, Reel 20.

[26]"How the War News is Received," *New York Tribune,* 16 April 1861, p. 5.

[27]Proclamation Calling Militia and Convening Congress, 15 April 1861, Abraham Lincoln Papers, Reel 20.

[28]Sandburg, *Abraham Lincoln—The War Years,* 214.

[29]John Tyler to Julia Tyler, 16 April 1861, John Tyler Papers, Reel 2, Series 1.

[30]Franklin Pierce to Martin Van Buren, 16 April 1861, Martin Van Buren Papers, Series 2, Reel 34.

[31] Martin Van Buren to Franklin Pierce, 20 April 1861, Martin Van Buren Papers, Series 2, Reel 34.

INDEX